For Katie and Dan

Stephen Golding is Senior Chaplain to Christ's
Hospital School in West Sussex, England.

## Acknowledgements

I would like to thank those who have given helpful
feedback and encouragement during the writing of
this book. Many thanks to Rhea Babla for the cover
design and to Amelia Hart for her help with the
illustrations. These were created by Maddy Ebbrell,
Andréa Barbeau, Megan Whitney, Lucy Ramshaw,
Mollie Brown, Leah Samuel, Tvesa Patel and Adela-
Marie Seeley, all pupils at Christ's Hospital School.

**Reality**

good
evil
beauty
pain
suffering
love
joy
tears
life
death

**Meaning?**

# Contents

## Starters

## Signs

## Questions

## Connections

# Starters

# An Open Mind?

## Human Story 1: Rough Justice

The suspect had been arrested, charged and convicted. She was known to have a violent temper. She had been spotted at the scene of the crime. The jury was persuaded: she was guilty of murder; but her innocence was later established and the murderer was never discovered.

## Human Story 2: Mental Shift

For hundreds and thousands of years people believed that the earth stood still and the sun moved across the sky. It was easy to feel confident in such a belief, all you had to do was look and the truth was plain to see. The sun rises in the east and everyone can see that as the day passes, it moves across the sky to set in the west.

It came as something of a surprise when people like the astronomer Galileo showed that the old way of seeing things was mistaken. What had seemed obvious to everyone for so long had to give way to the unexpected truth that it was the earth that moved and not the sun.

There was quite a struggle at the time. Galileo was arrested and put under pressure to deny what he knew to be true. People's minds did not easily change. The truth was surprising and alarming. The obvious answer turned out to be the wrong answer.

## Human Story 3: Conversion Experience

C.S. Lewis taught at both Oxford and Cambridge Universities and is well known for his children's stories set in the magical land of Narnia. He wrote his own life story and called it, "Surprised by Joy". In it he describes how he came to change his mind about God:

*"I became aware that I was holding something at bay, or shutting something out. .... I felt myself being, there and then, given a free choice. I could open the door or keep it shut; .... I chose to open, .... I felt as if I were a man of snow at long last beginning to melt."*

## Human Story 4: Missing Body

Jesus' life began with surprises. The Wise Men from the East expected to find him at the palace in the capital city, but they were led to a more surprising destination. The rest of Jesus' life was no less unusual and the end of the story was far from predictable. He was executed and buried on a Friday. One of his friends visited his grave on the following Sunday morning and found the cave-like tomb empty.

The explanation was obvious, someone had moved the body to another tomb, but what she was confronted with turned her world on its head.

*"Mary turned round and saw Jesus standing there, but she did not realise that it was Jesus. ... Thinking he was the gardener, she said, "Sir, if you have carried him away, tell me where you have put him, and I will get him." Jesus said to her, "Mary." (Gospel of John)*

The obvious answer was the wrong answer.

The truth was far more surprising and exciting.

---

**Follow the evidence wherever it leads**

The search for what is true and real is not easy. It requires time and effort and a willingness to question the spirit of the age in which we live and the things we have been told. This can be uncomfortable. The truth might not be what we want it to be, but if we genuinely want to know what is real, we will have to accept what we find, whether we like it or not.

# Faith

The history books tell us that something amazing happened in 1969. Human beings travelled to the moon! But do we know that it really happened? People claim to know because they can look at and listen to the evidence. They can read newspapers from the time; they can look at film footage or listen to eyewitness accounts. Once they have the evidence they can weigh it up and see if it is strong enough to persuade them.

In science there is a similar kind of process. We can do experiments and read about other people's experiments and then decide whether or not the evidence supports the idea that has been suggested.

Most of what we claim to know about history or science, we have taken on trust from teachers, books, the television or the internet. Usually we have not carried out the experiments or spoken to eyewitnesses ourselves.

What about knowing that someone loves you? Again, it is not a matter of 100% proof; it is a case of being persuaded by experience. They show you affection, they do things for you and on the basis of this evidence you trust that they really do care about you.

In every area of life, there are things that we know, not because we have proof, but by deciding whether or not the evidence is convincing enough. If it is, we are willing to believe.

14

Faith is in fact something we are using every day, all of the time.

Imagine a person who has no faith, a person who will not trust:

*The alarm clock rang and John wearily opened his eyes. The clock said 7.00 a.m. but John was worried. What if the clock had stopped in the night and restarted again? He put the radio on to get a second opinion. Having pulled on some clothes, he washed and shaved.*

*John had written a letter the night before and so after breakfast he set off for work via the post box. He turned the corner and there it was in front of him, a red column with a slit opening. If he put the letter in, it may never be seen again, how did he know that someone would collect it and that it would ever be delivered? He pulled back his hand just in time and decided to deliver it himself.*

*The morning went slowly but at last it was lunchtime. John took out his homemade sandwiches and munched through them. He never ate in the canteen; after all you could not be sure that the caterers were not messing around with the food. They might have put all sorts of things in the rice pudding.*

*After work he met someone he knew coming out of the dentists. John had not been to the dentist for years. He just could not understand how anyone could trust a stranger to poke sharp instruments around the inside of their mouth!*

15

Jude

*On the way home he delivered his letter. It was to his fiancée, calling off the engagement. He could not go ahead with it because he could not be totally sure that she really loved him. How could he know for certain that she was not seeing someone else?*

*John arrived home feeling rather depressed. Why could not life involve less risk? Why did everything have to demand so much trust?* Otto

Every day we believe a hundred and one things that we cannot prove. Every day we trust other people in all sorts of ways. Every day we believe in things we have never seen for ourselves. Faith is at the heart of our everyday lives. We are all believers. Afie

\*

Charles Blondin was a famous tightrope walker in the nineteenth century. He was best known for his amazing high wire walks across the Niagara Falls. He made it look easy, but then he would call for volunteers to be carried across on his back or in a wheelbarrow.

Believing that Blondin was an amazing tightrope walker was not difficult. People could see for themselves his extraordinary talent, but when he asked people to trust him to carry them across the wire, that was a different story.

Lots believed, few trusted. In the same way, most people believe that there is a God, but what if God is looking for people who will weigh up the evidence and take, not a leap in the dark, but a personal step of trust.

16

## Seeing is Believing?

All around us there is an unseen world rich in music and drama, sport and conversation. You cannot see it, but it really is there if only you can connect with it. If you have a radio you can tune in and expand your horizons and enrich your life.

*

Have you ever seen an idea, a thought, a mind?

Do you believe in gravity and subatomic particles?

*

- Is it natural to believe in God?

- If you stopped believing in God, was there a good reason?

- Do people who believe in God have more faith than those who do not, or is it the other way round?

- Is being willing to believe as important as having reasons to believe?

- Do people just believe what they want to believe?

- Can faith exist without doubt or are they two sides of the same coin?

17

# The Search

There was a wealthy young man who had made his fortune as a diamond trader. He worked long hours seeking out and buying beautiful diamonds and then selling them on at a handsome profit. He was good at what he did and his work was his life. He knew the slogans well: 'Diamonds are forever', 'Diamonds are a girl's best friend.'

One day an agent he had never met before came to his office with an exciting proposal. 'I know of a gem of enormous and unparalleled value that can be yours if you are willing to search it out.' Tempted by such a prize the young man enquired where he might find this precious jewel. 'I'm sure you know where to go', said the messenger.

So after some thought he packed his bags and set off for the diamond capital of the world and to the headquarters of the biggest of all the traders. As you would expect they had plenty of gems to show him, but there was nothing that excited him, nothing exceptional.

And so feeling rather disappointed he checked into a sumptuous hotel and then into the restaurant for a meal. As he looked around the other tables, to his surprise, there was the agent he had met just a few days ago. He approached him irritably. 'You said there was a gem of extraordinary value that would be mine if I would search it out. Well I've come to the diamond *capital of the world and they haven't shown me anything that fits your description.'*

*The agent was unruffled by this news and handed the young man a small folded piece of paper. He unfolded the scrap and found on it a series of numbers. Back in his room he typed the code into the search engine on his laptop. He discovered that they were grid references and continuing the search they gave him an address. He felt the kick of excitement that he had known many times before when a lucrative deal was beckoning. 'So that's where I'll find this priceless jewel.'*

*The following day he took a taxi to the place he had been shown. To his surprise he was deposited outside a simple and rather shabby Guest House in a non-descript part of town. 'Are you sure this is right?' 'This is the place you asked for', said the driver.*

*So the young man entered the Guest House and at the reception they seemed to be expecting him. 'They're waiting for you', he was told.*

*Apprehensively the young man turned the key in the door he had been directed to and there to his surprise stood the three people in the world that he counted as his friends; the friends he had been too busy to see for months now. 'What are you doing here?' he spluttered. 'We were rushed here last night. They told us that you needed us to be here if you are to find what you're looking for.' 'But I was told that if I came here I'd find a gem of great value. It's supposed to be of incomparable worth. Is it here?'*

*At that moment the phone beside the bed rang. The young man answered it and recognised the voice. It was the agent who had set him off on this search in the first place. 'Now you listen to me', said the young man, his voice raised in a threatening tone. 'You told me that I would find a gem of incomparable worth. I've come to where you said and it's not here.'*

*There was a brief silence at the other end of the phone. And then a calm voice replied, 'You know the price, but you have forgotten the value.'*

*Suddenly he felt dizzy and the room seemed to swim before him. And in those moments of confusion everything in the room became distorted. His friends seemed to shrink and become tiny figures before him and as he looked he saw himself in the mirror and he too was a tiny figure, bowed down and obscured by a ridiculously large diamond that he held in his hands. All of his energy and attention seemed to be taken up with keeping hold of that huge stone. And the quiet voice said to him, 'A fool knows the price but not the value. What you seek is here but not what you expected.'*

*The young man reached out to steady himself. The room returned to normal and yet everything now looked different. What had seemed to matter so much, now seemed small and narrow, but friendship appeared wide and deep and without price.*

# Mystery

On the 5th of December 1872 Captain David
Moorhouse was sailing 600 miles west of Gibralter
when the erratic movements of another vessel, the
Mary Celeste, caught his attention. A boarding party
was dispatched to investigate and they found the ship
was strangely silent. It was intact and there was no
evidence of violence, but the crew had completely
disappeared. The reason for their disappearance has
never been discovered.

A mystery involves something unexplained, something
hidden and unsolved. Mysteries fascinate us.

**Try a thought experiment:**

Imagine a time machine. You climb in and travel back
in time. You pass through millions of years and
eventually come to the 'Big Bang', the great explosion
that threw out the stars and planets of the universe. You
have reached the beginning, but can your time machine
keep going? What happens next? Can you travel back
before the Big Bang or does time itself begin there?

Here lies a big question: Is it possible for the matter or
energy of the universe to be eternal? Did it begin to
exist or could it have always been there with no
beginning?

When you think back in time you are not left with
many options. Either the stuff of the universe is eternal;
or it just appeared from nowhere; or, if there is a creator

who brought everything else into being, the creator would be eternal and would never have had a beginning. Whatever you believe, all of this is beyond our grasp; all of the options are mysterious.

Thinking about space has the same unsettling effect.

Imagine going up in a spaceship. Imagine you just keep going, up and up and up. Could you ever come to the edge of the universe and if so, what would be on the other side?

When we ask the big questions about the physical universe, about space and time, we are left with things that are beyond our imaginations.

The universe is mysterious and a God who made it would be even more so.

# The Bridge

*Imagine a wide gorge, a deep, steep sided valley. Imagine you are standing on one side of the gorge and as you look across, it is so far that it is hard to see the land opposite. And imagine that up on one side of this gorge there is a village.*

*It was said in that village that there had once been a bridge across to the other side. And it was said that on the other side of this deep and wide gorge there was a garden where the gardener grew wonderful fruit trees. An ancient story said that people who ate the fruit of those trees were filled with joy and love and life.*

*But sadly, long ago the bridge across the gorge had been broken down and no-one had ever been able to rebuild it. It had happened such a long time ago that a lot of people had started to say that there never had been a bridge across the gorge. Some were starting to say that there never was a garden or any fruit. Some of the older folk could remember people trying to build a bridge, but no-one had ever succeeded in reaching the other side.*

*And then one day a visitor arrived in the village. At first the people welcomed him and they wanted to know where he had come from and what he could tell them of things he had seen and heard on his travels. But when he started to say that he was 'The Master Bridge Builder' and that his father was 'The Gardener' and that he had come from across the gorge and that his Father had sent him to rebuild the ancient bridge, some people turned against him and started to say that he was mad.*

*'I've come to build you a bridge so that you can be friends with The Gardener again and eat his fruit,' he would say.*

*'We are happy as we are, we don't need your help,' they replied, 'if we want a bridge we'll build it ourselves.'*

*'But you won't be able to build a bridge that can cross such a wide and deep gorge. It's too far to the other side and it's too deep.'*

*'There's nothing on the other side anyway,' said someone in the crowd. 'There is no gardener. Go back to where you came from; we didn't invite you here anyway.'*

*But the Bridge Builder was very determined. He took them to the edge of the gorge and showed them exactly where the bridge would be built. Then he told them a riddle, and it went like this:*

*'The bridge that I build will really be, but only with trust will you be able to see.'*

*The more he talked about being sent to build a bridge, the more angry some of the people became. 'Lots of people have tried to build a bridge to the other side and no-one's managed it yet. Who does he think he is? Does he think he can do something that no-one else has been able to do?'*

*In fact some of the people got so angry that they started to plot how they might silence the Bridge Builder for ever. 'We'll throw him into the gorge then we won't have to listen to him anymore,' they said.*

*That night when there was no moon in the sky and it was very dark they came to where The Gardener's son was staying. They tied him up and took him to a high place on the edge of the gorge and they threw him over the cliff and into the darkness below.*

*But they had forgotten the words of the old prophecy:*

*'Into the gorge my son they will throw,*
*but let everyone listening know:*
*on the day that he dies*
*the ancient bridge will arise.'*

*With the Bridge Builder gone the people thought that life would now return to normal. But it was not to be. Just days later a child in the village said that she had been across the gorge and had met with The Gardener. The elders looked out across the gorge. There was no bridge to be seen. 'Just a silly child making up stories', they said as they turned away and went back to their homes.*

*They had gone when another child came and stood at the edge of the gorge. And the child put his foot out over the edge right at the place where the Bridge*

*Builder had said that the bridge would be. It looked as if he would fall into the gorge, but he did not fall. Instead he started to walk across the gorge as if he were walking in mid-air, as if he were walking on a bridge that no-one could see.*

*So it was that those who were willing to trust in the Bridge Builder's invisible bridge walked across the gorge and ate The Gardener's fruit. And when they came back they tried to tell everyone about the things they had seen and the fruit they had tasted. The others however, would not believe them, but they could not help noticing that those who claimed to have been across the bridge seemed to have tasted something real and kind and joyful.*

# Signs

# Only Natural?

Many people are worried about our natural environment. Creatures are threatened with extinction and water, air and land are troubled by pollution. We know as never before that animals and plants live in carefully balanced ecosystems. If one creature is removed others suffer. If one part is damaged there are consequences elsewhere.

Science shows us that nature is made up of organised working systems.

Our own bodies are an example of this, with several inter-related systems that work together to enable us to live. Our blood supply, digestive system and lungs deliver food and oxygen to every part of the body. Muscles, nerves and bones work together to allow us to move. Our sense organs need co-ordination from the brain. Waste products have to be dealt with, and all of these systems are encoded in the information contained in our genes.

Like eco-systems, our bodies are made up of organised inter-related systems and these systems are purposeful, they make life possible.

Experience teaches us that organised systems are evidence of intelligence. Think of a school timetable. It works because intelligent thought has been put into it. In life it takes thought to create order; to achieve organisation and purpose you need intelligent input. So what about the natural world?

The DNA in our cells carries the information that can be translated into the biology of our bodies and we normally assume that this kind of programming is achieved by intelligent activity.

Could the working systems we see in nature and the coded instructions of DNA be clues to the existence of a mind that works in and through natural processes to achieve what it intends?

Living things have the amazing capacity to change, adapt and evolve. Evolution is a clever system by which increasingly complex creatures have developed and conscious, intelligent beings have come into existence. The process looks as if it has been designed to produce a world of diverse and amazing plants and animals.

Perhaps you have found yourself wondering whether the design you see in nature suggests an intelligent mind, a Creator.

There are several aspects of the natural world that especially point to a creative intelligence:

- The 'laws of nature' – the natural world behaves in a rational way. It works according to predictable mathematical patterns. Nature is governed by the kind of rules that you would expect a rational mind to create.

- The language of genes – the DNA in every cell of our bodies carries a purposeful coded message. It is like a set of instructions that a person might write.

- The process of evolution – this seems to be set up to produce increasingly complex organisms including intelligent creatures that are spiritually and morally aware. It is as if someone had a purpose they were aiming to achieve.

- The organised systems within nature – order, organisation and purpose are what you expect when intelligence is at work.

- The minds of human beings – we can think and reason things out. We believe that the truth matters. The fact that we are rational creatures would not be surprising if a rational mind created us. Closetotnum.com

As well as all of this, there are also a number of things about the way our universe works that are just right for life to evolve. It is as if a series of dials have been precisely set in order to fine-tune our universe so that life possible. The force of gravity is just one example of these cosmic coincidences. If the pull of gravity was a little stronger or weaker we would not be here. Like in the story of Goldilocks and the Three Bears, it is not too strong and not too weak but just right.

Why should this be? We could say that it is just a very lucky chance that the universe is the way it is. Alternatively, we could suggest that for some unknown

31

Mystery.
Intelligible +
beautiful

Does the universe
have a meaning/
purpose? What is it?

reason, the universe has to be this way. Some speculate that there must be lots of universes and ours is the one that happens to have the right conditions.

But what if there is a creative Mind who wanted living things to evolve? That would explain why the universe has just the right conditions for life.

Most scientists agree that the process of evolution explains how the living things of our world have developed, but this still leaves the big question: Does the universe and the process of evolution just exist, or do they exist because there is a Creator who wanted living things to develop and evolve in this way? And this question still remains even if there are lots of universes.

> What do you think?
> Does the natural world point beyond itself, to a Mind, an eternal intelligence that is responsible for the space and time of this material universe?

If there is a creative intelligence behind the natural world there are still plenty of questions to ask. Is this intelligence good, or evil, or both? Is it all-powerful, or limited; a single mind, or many minds?

Lots of questions remain, but the world around us seems to cry out for an explanation from beyond itself. The natural world does not seem to be a brute fact; it suggests something greater than itself and invites us to search out what, or who it is pointing to.

Do the fine-tuning of the universe; the process of evolution that gives rise to living, thinking creatures; the laws of nature; the language of genes and the organised systems of the natural world, point beyond themselves to an intelligent creative Mind?

*Maddy*

# Who Created God?

Experience teaches us that everything that happens has a cause. We talk about 'cause and effect' and scientists devote themselves to studying this in the natural world. Could the universe be an eternal sequence of cause and effect that has no beginning?

We can talk hypothetically about the idea of an eternal sequence of events, but it is questionable whether such a thing could actually exist. If the universe goes back in time forever, would today ever arrive?

Or to put it another way: We know that everything that begins to exist has a cause; otherwise we would have to believe in some kind of magic. We would have to believe that something could come from nothing.

If the universe began to exist, it must have been caused by something.

A Mind that exists outside of time and intended the universe to be there and brought it into being, would explain why there is a universe.

Of course this leaves us with a God who is not bound by time and has always existed, but to ask, 'who created God?' is not a meaningful question. It is asking, 'who created the uncreated creator? Or, 'when did the timeless one begin?' It is like asking a person who has always been honest, 'when did you stop lying?'

Some questions just do not make sense.

# Home Alone?

We are told that genetically speaking there is only about a 2% difference between chimpanzees and ourselves. Just 2% makes us distinctively human.

So what difference does that 2% make? What is it that distinguishes us from other primates? Is it our intelligence and our ability to communicate? Is it our curiosity, self-consciousness, creativity and ability to set long term goals? Is it our sense of right and wrong and our ability to worship and pray?

We are exceptional, but were we ever intended? Did anyone plan for us to be here or did we arrive in the universe by accident?

We know what it is to love and to be hurt. We have hopes and fears and we can ask questions about the purpose of our lives, but according to the atheist philosopher Bertrand Russell this is all the product of luck (or bad luck):

*"Man is the product of causes which had no prevision of the end they were achieving; ... his origin, his growth, his hopes and fears, his loves and beliefs, are but the outcome of accidental collocations of atoms."*

If we are the result of physical processes alone then there is no over-arching purpose to our lives. Ultimately there is no reason for which we exist, there is no plan, no bigger picture. No-one intended for us to be here. We are alone in an impersonal universe; persons in an impersonal, material world.

All of this is rather disappointing, but there is an alternative. What if there is a personal Creator? What if there is a God who cares about us and made us for a reason, a God who created us so that we could know him and love him and live as his agents, in his world, in caring relationships with all that he has made? If this is true then we are at home in the universe, we are persons in a meaningful world. The universe is purposeful, not merely material and ultimately meaningless.

As you pass people in the street or look in the mirror, what do you see: the accidental products of nature or those made by a Creator who loves and cares?

One Bible writer says this: *"When I consider your heavens, the work of your fingers, the moon and the stars, which you have set in place, what is mankind that you are mindful of them, human beings that you care for them?*

*You have made them a little lower than the angels and crowned them with glory and honour." (Psalm 8)*

This is rather more hopeful than the atheist belief that human beings are alone in a merely material, impersonal and indifferent universe.

Is there something about being a human person that points beyond itself?

We are spiritual as well as material. Could our own existence be a sign of some greater reality?

Human beings experience

physical hunger

...... and there is food.


Human beings experience

physical thirst

...... and there is water.


Human beings experience

spiritual hunger and thirst

..... and there is _____?

*Andréa*

# The Centre

Many people in the world live tough lives. Each day is a struggle for survival and surviving itself is for them the centre of their life. All of their activities are geared to this one controlling principle, the need to survive. To some extent this is true for all of us. We eat, drink, sleep and keep warm in order to survive.

Thankfully though, for many of us life is not just a struggle to stay alive. We have some choice of career and we have leisure time, we have some choice of friends, some spare money and a choice as to how we spend it. We can choose how we spend some of our time, money and energy and these choices show what is really important to us.

For many people, image is clearly very important and they spend a lot of time, creating and maintaining their chosen style. For all of us happiness is clearly a key goal, and for many it is family or friends that matter most. Consciously or unconsciously we all choose the centre around which our life revolves. Once the centre is fixed our lifestyle follows.

If someone was to study your life, what would they conclude from the way you spend your energy, time and money? What do you think they would say is at the hub of your wheel? What is at the centre of your concerns, what are the organising principles of your life-style?

Jesus suggested that two things make for a properly centred life: firstly, love for God and secondly, love for others. 'Love God with your whole self and love others like you love yourself' was his answer to the question of what matters most in life.

According to Jesus this is the meaning of our lives as human beings. It is as we look outwards, as we broaden our horizons and open our lives to these two controlling principles that we find the reason for which we were created. Strangely, we find ourselves and our fulfilment and meaning as we lose ourselves in love for God and for others.

Imagine a graph that you might draw in maths or science. A point on the graph is useless unless there are two labelled axes to tell you what it means. With these two axes to refer to, the point on the graph can have a meaning and a value. It is as if we are a point on a graph and we are trying to work out what we mean and what our value is. According to Jesus, the answer is found as we look at the two axes of love for God and love for others.

# It's Personal

What do you feel really strongly about? What makes you angry? When you read or hear about people being treated unfairly because of their colour or gender or political beliefs, is there something in you that wants to shout out, 'That's wrong, that's not fair, that's not the way it ought to be'? And when you see people suffering because of poverty or some other misfortune do you find your heart going out to them? Do you want to help them and put things right?

Why do human beings feel so strongly about love and justice?

Imagine yourself in a school playground. Small children are all around you playing all kinds of games. It will not be long before you hear someone say, 'That's not fair' or 'But you promised' or 'Stop pushing in'.

We all seem to believe in a set of rules by which everyone ought to behave.

If you want to challenge someone about what they have done, what do you say? Probably something like, 'That was really selfish' or, 'That was really unfair.' And if someone challenges us like this we usually try to claim that we were not really being selfish or unfair at all. We do not say, 'Being selfish or unfair does not matter.' We are aware of right and wrong and we all seem to appeal to some over-arching set of rules and values. We all believe in good and evil.

And we are not just products of the society we live in. Many people have felt compelled to speak out against the social order of their day, think of Martin Luther King and Nelson Mandela for example. We seem to believe in standards against which we can judge the way we have been brought up and the society we are part of.

We act as if injustice and selfishness are obviously wrong. We experience a sense of outrage if we are treated unfairly and we know what it is to feel ashamed of falling short. We experience guilt. Human beings are not morally neutral. We have a conscience and feel that we ought to behave in certain ways.

Why are we like this?

What if the universe exists just because it always has and we have developed out of material things by physical processes alone? An impersonal, material universe could not care less about what we do. Atoms and molecules do not care about justice or love. Matter is amoral. The material universe is not interested in whether you are the worst of sinners or the best of saints and yet we all believe in right and wrong and in love and justice.

So is there a different way of seeing things? What if there is a Creator who cares about things being right and fair?

If the intelligence that made the universe is a moral being who cares about right and wrong, that would explain why human beings are like that too.

Does our belief in love and justice point beyond itself and invite us to ask whether the universe is a moral as well as a material place?

Human beings are persons not just material objects.

Human beings recognise the difference between right and wrong.

Human beings believe in love and justice.

Does all of this point beyond itself to a personal and moral being who made us personal and moral beings too?

# Do you agree ...?

**Step 1.** Do you agree that good people should be happier than bad people?

If you agree go to step 2.

**Step 2.** Do you agree that bad people sometimes seem to be as happy, or happier than, good people?

If you agree go to step 3.

**Step 3.** Do you agree that if there is a good God, justice can ultimately be done because God will make sure that happiness and goodness go together?

If you agree go to step 4.

**Step 4.** Is it therefore necessary to believe in God if goodness and happiness are to coincide and justice is to be done in the end?

# Experience

You can know something about swimming by watching other people swim or by reading all about it in a book, but it is only when you get into the water that you really know what swimming is.

Many people believe that they know God in this direct kind of way. If you asked them why they believe in God they would not give a philosophical kind of answer. They would speak about their own personal experience.

These experiences are of various kinds. Some people have what would be called a conversion experience. Something happens that turns their life around and leads them to faith. The most famous conversion experience is in the Bible itself and involves Paul of Tarsus, (also known as Saul). He had been an active enemy of the Christian faith, but something happened that turned his life around and led him to spread the Christian message instead. His experience happened as he travelled from Jerusalem to Damascus and it left him temporarily blind. It is described like this:

*"About noon as I came near Damascus, suddenly a bright light from heaven flashed around me. I fell to the ground and heard a voice say to me, 'Saul! Saul! Why do you persecute me?'*

*'Who are you, Lord?' I asked. 'I am Jesus of Nazareth, whom you are persecuting,' he replied. My companions saw the light, but they did not understand the voice of*

*him who was speaking to me. 'What shall I do, Lord?' I asked. 'Get up,' the Lord said, 'and go into Damascus. There you will be told all that you have been assigned to do.' My companions led me by the hand into Damascus, because the brilliance of the light had blinded me." (The Acts of the Apostles)*

Most people do not have such dramatic experiences, but there are modern day examples of those who claim to have had life changing spiritual encounters like this.

Others will speak of sensing the reality and closeness of God through music and during worship. Many find prayer to be a meaningful way of connecting with God. There are also those who would claim surprising answers to their prayers in terms of healing or the provision of urgently needed resources.

It is possible to experience being filled with the love of God and flooded with a sense of God's peace and joy.

There can be moments when it seems obvious that there is more to life than merely the material; that beyond the world we know through our senses there is a reality that we connect with in our spirit.

Human beings are spiritual beings and spiritual experiences are part of our human story. Lots of people could be deluded, but on the other hand it could be that those who do not have such experiences are missing out on something really important.

- **Imagine a life without music.**

It would be possible to live such a life and to be happy enjoying other things, but a life without music would be less than it could be.

If you took such a person to a concert or gave them some music to listen to they would suddenly realize that they had been living in a silent world that lacked something life-giving and important.

- **Imagine a life without faith, prayer and God.**

It would be possible to live such a life and to be happy enjoying other things, but would a life without God be less than it could be?

## A Subconscious Need?

Some suggest that we invent God because we have a subconscious longing for a father figure to comfort and protect us from the insecurities of life.

If this is true then faith is just a kind of psychological crutch to help us cope and we need to grow up and face reality with a bit more courage.

The problem with this kind of speculation however, is that it can easily be turned on its head.

What if rejection of God is due to a subconscious desire to get rid of him and to break free and live our lives our own way?

If this is true then we need to grow out of this childish rebellion and face up to the reality that God exists.

And what if belief in God brings security and comfort because God really is there and really does care about us?

And belief in God is not just about comfort and security. Faith responds to a demanding challenge: the call to put aside my own wishes and to allow God's will to be done in my life, however difficult that might be.

# Hope

Can the future change the present? It clearly can. Think of how the prospect of an examination next week can spoil your weekend! Knowing that you have an interview or a hospital appointment tomorrow can completely change how you feel today. Looking forward to going out with someone or going on holiday makes all the difference to the mundane work that has to be done in the meantime.

But what about the longer term future? Do our beliefs about what happens to us after we die make a difference to how we feel about life and how we live now?

John Lennon's famous lyrics encourage us to "Imagine there's no heaven, it's easy if you try." Bertrand Russell was sure that this life is all there is, "When I die I shall rot", he said. But Christians believe that death is not the end.

But why do Christians believe this? I suppose it is difficult to accept that the people we love are just going to disappear when they die and it is hard to imagine ourselves no longer existing. There is also the uncomfortable thought that if death is the end, life can seem, in the bigger scheme of things, a bit pointless. On their own though, these reasons might look like wishful thinking.

Jesus however, gave a stronger reason for believing. He not only taught that death is not the end, he proved it by outliving death himself.

Jesus proved that the death barrier could be broken.

Christians believe in a future for individuals and they also believe that the history of the world is going somewhere too. What a contrast again with Bertrand Russell who believed that *"all the labours of the ages, all the devotion, all the inspiration, all the noonday brightness of human genius, are destined to extinction in the vast death of the solar system."*

Compare his view with the hope for the future expressed in the last book of the Bible: *"Then I saw a new heaven and a new earth ... And I heard a loud voice from the throne saying, 'Look! God's dwelling place is now among the people, and he will dwell with them ... and be their God. He will wipe every tear from their eyes. There will be no more death or mourning or crying or pain, for the old order of things has passed away.'"*

So, what of our individual future and what of the future of the world? Where are we heading? And does that future give us hope and change the present?

The idea of a 'Day of Judgment' after we die can sound negative, but strangely it is good news.

Jesus believed in such a day. He did not give many details, but he used two pictures to talk about it and he gave really serious warnings telling us to make sure we end up in the right place.

One picture he used was of a grim kind of graveyard just outside Jerusalem.

Anyone in their right mind would not want to spend any time there. Jesus talks about weeping, sadness and regret and warns us in the most serious terms, of a future to be avoided.

His other picture is of a great party, a party not to be missed. It is a picture of happiness, friendship, belonging, and fulfillment.

Jesus invites us to be at the party, not in the graveyard. He meant it to be a stark contrast.

So how is the 'Day of Judgment' good news? It is certainly good for those who join the party but it is good news in two other ways as well.

Firstly, it means that evil people will not get away with it in the end. We all hate injustice, but people will never be called to account if there is no final judgment by God. If things are to be fair there has to be some kind of day of reckoning beyond this life.

Secondly, it means that the kind of person we are really matters. If it is true that the destiny of the solar system and everything in it is merely an inferno or a frozen waste, then in the end no-one is going to care whether you were Nelson Mandela or Adolf Hitler. If there is no God who stands as our Judge, there is no-one to finally say that a generous life was better than a cruel one.

51

The Christian faith says that the kind of person I am and the way I live really matters, because it matters to God.

What we believe about our own future individually and about the future of the world changes how we see life today.

The future we believe in does indeed change the present.

# The Ticket

*Four teenagers, two boys, two girls found themselves together on a train journey. At first they sat quietly but the journey was long and so after a while they got talking. One of them, a young man of about seventeen wearing a T-shirt with a slogan that read "Let's Party" turned to one of the girls. "So where are you going?" he asked. "Oh, I don't know" she replied, "my parents put me on the train but I don't know where it's going and the strange thing is, they didn't seem to know either." She looked a bit anxious and kept peering out of the window in order to find some clues about the train's destination. She was wearing a T-shirt much like the boy's only hers read, "Don't Ask Me!" "But it's not going anywhere" interrupted the other girl in the carriage, "Just enjoy the journey". She was wearing a slogan too and it was rather longer, "It's not the winning but the taking part that counts."*

*"You mean you don't think that there is any destination, any station at the end of the line at all?" said the young man. He kept glancing out of the window as if he expected to arrive somewhere any time now. He was like a child in the back seat of the car who keeps asking 'are we there yet?' "People need to believe in a destination, but that's just wishful thinking if you ask me" the girl replied. "They just can't face the fact that the journey is all that we've got. Engineers can tell us how this train was made; they can explain how it works. We know all about it, all that talk about a station at the end of the line, it's just pie in the sky."*

*The other passenger was sitting quietly, deep in thoughtful meditation. His T-shirt simply read "Déjà vu". "I've been here before", he said. You see the mistake you are making is to think that the train runs along a line from one place to another. The train is on a circuit, it goes round and round. I've been round several times." He gazed out of the window and looked at the clear sky. "One day I'm going to escape the train and leave my body behind and fly away."*

*The "Let's Party!" young man looked at the other three. "Strange isn't it", he said. "Here we are on the same train. We can see the landscape going by and we can remember places we've been but it's as if we've all got different tickets."*

*The young man looked at his ticket and held it out to the others. "It looks more like an invitation" he said, and as they looked at the tickets in their hands the train seemed to slow down and very faintly somewhere in the distance they thought they might have heard what sounded like a wild kind of music.*

# Paradox

Maximilian Kolbe died in 1941 in Auschwitz, the notorious Nazi concentration camp. The Nazis had chosen ten men to be starved to death as a reprisal because three prisoners had escaped. Kolbe had not been chosen, but hearing one of the men crying out that he would never see his wife and children again, he stepped forward and took the man's place. He was forty-seven years old and with the other nine he died slowly without food or water.

What a contrast there is between the cruelty of the Nazis and the self-sacrificing concern of Maximilian Kolbe.

This story highlights in an extreme and stark way the paradox of our human nature. People can be kind, generous and creative and yet they can also be cruel, selfish and destructive.

If we know ourselves we will have found the same contradiction in our own hearts and minds. In the same day we can show real concern for others and yet we can also be unkind and hurtful. In the same hour we can think good thoughts as well as thoughts that we would be embarrassed to have others hear.

Individually and as a human race we are a confusing combination of qualities to be admired and failings that make us ashamed. This is who we are. C. S. Lewis expressed it well in one of his Narnia stories:

*"You come of the Lord Adam and the Lady Eve. And that is both honour enough to erect the head of the poorest beggar, and shame enough to bow the shoulders of the greatest emperor on earth."*

If we are going to be realistic, we need an understanding of human nature that enables us to hold on to our greatness while facing up to our shame.

The Bible story tells us that we are each of great value and dignity because we are all created by God.

A Van Gogh painting will fetch a fortune at auction because of who created it. Similarly, we are worth a great deal because of who made us.

And not only that, we are made like God, we reflect his image and share his qualities of intelligence, creativity and moral and spiritual awareness, in a way that no other creature does.

And, as if that were not enough, God also loves us, so much so that he came to the world as Jesus to win our friendship.

The other side of the coin is of course less appealing to us. The same story tells us that we rebel against God, we ignore God, we hide from him and we go our own way, sometimes through weakness, sometimes by deliberate choice. Instead of opening ourselves out in love for God and for others, we so readily close in on ourselves and indulge our selfishness.

We are a paradox of honour and shame and we need a way of looking at life that helps us to make sense of both aspects of our human nature. We need a philosophy of life that helps us to understand who we really are.

*Megan*

**Have you ever ...**

... been filled with a sense of wonder?

... been moved by beauty?

... been disturbed by the pain in the world?

... felt the joy of friendship?

... been moved with compassion?

... been angry at injustice?

... wondered what life is for?

... been in love?

... felt spiritually empty?

... felt a longing for a being who is greater than this world?

... wanted to pray?

... wanted to say 'thank you'?

... felt accountable for what you think or do or say?

... felt a longing for a bigger meaning to your life?

... rebelled against the idea that death is
the end of someone you love?

Could these feelings be drawing you towards something
bigger and deeper, towards a reality beyond this world?

# The One

Films have been made about him, paintings have been created, musicals have been sung, and countless books have been written. For millions upon millions of people he is an influence in their lives. Why is it that this man, who lived so long ago in a world so different to our own, holds so much significance for people all over the world today?

He was born in Roman times, to humble people in difficult circumstances. We know little of his early life. He is said to have performed miracles, to have taught with stories, to have died an ugly and brutal death, and it is claimed that after his death he was seen alive again. One of his early followers says this about him:

*"Jesus of Nazareth was a man accredited by God to you by miracles, wonders, and signs, which God did among you through him, as you yourselves know ... and you, with the help of wicked men, put him to death by nailing him to the cross. But God raised him from the dead, freeing him from the agony of death, because it was impossible for death to keep its hold on him." (Acts of the Apostles)*

What is it about Jesus that makes him so impressive and appealing to so many people?

Is it his power, the power to heal the sick, to banish evil from the disturbed, to raise the dead and to control the storm? If the accounts are reliable he certainly had power that no-one else has ever exercised.

Or is it perhaps his compassion that attracts us, his reaching out to those in need and to those who had lost their way? We see in him the kind of person we all know we should be, the kind of person we would like to be.

Or maybe it is his courage in challenging the establishment that appeals to us. His refusal to conform to rules, his challenging of the accepted ways of doing things.

We see him taken by his enemies, abused and beaten, but winning through in the end. Somehow he represents something that deep down we recognize and respond to. He suffers humiliation and pain but the story does not end there. Evil seems to triumph, but against all the odds, goodness has the final say. I wonder if it is his victory after apparent failure that draws us. So many stories, myths and films are based on this basic truth. There is something compelling in the innocent hero who suffers, seems to be beaten and yet finally rises to defeat the enemy. And so we see Jesus rise, alive again. Goodness wins in the end.

In the story of Jesus we see something that touches the heart of reality. We see enormous power made vulnerable. We see goodness die and yet live again.

Jesus' suffering and death seem to have an irresistible power. They act for us like a telescope allowing us to see hidden worlds.

As we look at him we see the suffering and the pain of God. We see the extent of God's love for us as he deals with the paradox of our human nature. We see how he loves us and yet how our alienation from him can only be solved at a painful cost. We see that we are loved to such an extent that God himself enters our world as a man executed on a cross.

# History

Jesus was a real historical figure as the following sources show.

### Three Non-Christian Sources

- **Cornelius Tacitus (c.55-117AD). Roman Historian.**

*"Nero ... treated with the most extreme punishments, some people, popularly known as Christians ... The originator of that name, Christus, had been executed when Tiberius was emperor by order of the procurator Pontius Pilatus."*

- **Flavius Josephus (c.37-100AD). Jewish Historian.**

Josephus says that King Herod executed John the Baptist (a story also recorded in the Gospels of Matthew and Mark) and he mentions Jesus' brother, James: *"He* [Annas the younger] *convened the court of the Sanhedrin, and brought before them the brother of Jesus the so-called Messiah, who was called James, and some other men, whom he accused of having broken the law, and handed them over to be stoned."*

There is also a longer section about Jesus:

*"About this time there lived Jesus, a wise man, if indeed one should call him a man. For he was a performer of astonishing deeds, a teacher of men who are happy to*

*accept the truth. He won over many Jews, and indeed also many Greeks. He was the Messiah. In response to a charge presented by the leading men among us, Pilatus condemned him to the cross; but those who had loved him at first did not give up, for he appeared to them on the third day alive again, as the prophets of God had spoken this and thousands of other wonders about him. And still to this day the tribe of Christians, named after him, has not disappeared."*

Josephus was not a Christian and Christians seem to have added to this passage, but there is little doubt that Josephus refers to Jesus as a figure of history.

- **Mara bar Serapion (Date of document uncertain, but possibly soon after 73AD).**

This prisoner of war from the Roman province of Syria wrote a letter to encourage his son to pursue wisdom. He argues that those who persecute the wise, suffer misfortune. He does not name Jesus directly, but it is reasonable to conclude that it is Jesus that he is talking about.

*"What advantage did the Athenians gain from putting Socrates to death? Famine and plague came upon them as a judgment for their crime. What advantage did the men of Samos gain from burning Pythagoras? In a moment their land was covered with sand. What advantage did the Jews gain from executing their wise King? It was just after that that their kingdom was abolished."*

## Four Christian Sources

The New Testament includes four Gospels. The majority of scholars agree that all four were written in the first century, the century in which Jesus lived. The exact dates are debated.

If we look at the manuscript evidence for the Gospels, we find that it is very strong compared with the evidence for other ancient writings. Take the great Greek philosopher, Plato, for example. The oldest copies of his writings come from hundreds of years after his death, whereas the oldest copies of the Gospels were produced a lot nearer to the events that they describe.

- **Matthew** emphasizes that Jesus fulfilled the Old Testament prophecies. A striking example of this is found in the prophet Isaiah chapter 53. This was written several hundred years before the time of Jesus, but it is as if the writer is speaking about his death:

*"He was despised and rejected by men, a man of sorrows, and familiar with suffering. Like one from whom men hide their faces he was despised, and we esteemed him not.*

*Surely he took up our infirmities and carried our sorrows, yet we considered him stricken by God, smitten by him and afflicted. But he was pierced for our transgressions, he was crushed for our iniquities; the punishment that brought us peace was upon him, and by his wounds we are healed. We all, like sheep, have gone astray, each of us has turned to his own way; and the Lord has laid on him the iniquity of us all."*

- **Mark** got his information from Peter, according to this very old tradition: *"Mark, who was the interpreter of Peter, wrote down accurately all that he remembered"* (Papias c.140 AD). Peter was one of Jesus' closest friends.

- **Luke** says that he carefully researched his information and used eye-witness accounts:

*"Many have undertaken to draw up an account of the things that have been fulfilled among us, just as they were handed down to us by those who from the first were eye-witnesses ... Therefore, since I myself have carefully investigated everything from the beginning, it seemed good also to me to write an orderly account for you ... so that you may know the certainty of the things you have been taught."*

- **John** records some of the miracles of Jesus and claims that:

*"Jesus did many other miraculous signs in the presence of his disciples, which are not recorded in this book. But these are written that you may believe that Jesus is the Christ, the Son of God, and that by believing you may have life in his name."*

# Light

Jesus came across a man who had been blind from birth *(See The Gospel of John chapter 9)*. Like many people at the time, his companions assumed that this was a punishment for the man's sins or for the sins of his parents. Jesus rejected this interpretation and then he did a remarkable thing – he healed the man who then returned home able to see!

*"His neighbours and those who had formerly seen him begging asked, "Isn't this the same man who used to sit and beg?" Some claimed that he was. Others said, "No, he only looks like him." But he himself insisted, "I am the man."*

The man's neighbours knew that blind people do not normally regain their sight like this! So they look for some other explanation, but the man insists that his sight has suddenly been restored and that it was Jesus who made it happen.

Jesus had healed the man on the holy day (the Sabbath) and the man's neighbours take him to the religious leaders. According to these religious leaders, healing is a kind of work and working was not allowed on the Sabbath. They are therefore not happy with what has happened.

*Some of the Pharisees said, "This man* [i.e. Jesus] *is not from God, for he does not keep the Sabbath." But others asked, "How can a sinner do such miraculous signs?" So they were divided.*

*Finally they turned again to the blind man, "What have you to say about him? It was your eyes he opened." The man replied, "He is a prophet." ... they sent for the man's parents. "Is this your son?" they asked. "Is this the one you say was born blind? How is it that now he can see?"*

*"We know he is our son," the parents answered, "and we know he was born blind. But how he can see now, or who opened his eyes, we don't know. Ask him. He is of age; he will speak for himself."*

*A second time they summoned the man who had been blind. "Give glory to God," they said. "We know this man is a sinner." He replied, "Whether he is a sinner or not, I don't know. One thing I do know. I was blind but now I see!" Then they asked him, "What did he do to you? How did he open your eyes?"*

*He answered, "I have told you already and you did not listen. Why do you want to hear it again? Do you want to become his disciples, too?"*

*Then they hurled insults at him and said, "You are this fellow's disciple! We are disciples of Moses! We know that God spoke to Moses, but as for this fellow, we don't even know where he comes from."*

*The man answered, "Now that is remarkable! You don't know where he comes from, yet he opened my eyes. ... Nobody has ever heard of opening the eyes of a man born blind. If this man were not from God, he could do nothing."*

The man who was blind is convinced that if Jesus can do this kind of miracle he must be from God. Meanwhile the religious leaders are faced with a dilemma. It seems that Jesus has done an amazing miracle, which would suggest that God is with him. However, he has also broken their religious rules, which makes them reject him.

Jesus found the blind man who could now see, and asked him, *"Do you believe in the Son of Man?"*

*"Who is he, sir?" the man asked. "Tell me so that I may believe in him." Jesus said, "You have now seen him; in fact, he is the one speaking with you." Then the man said, "Lord, I believe," and he worshipped him."*

Jesus challenges the man to follow through the implications of the miracle. If Jesus can do miracles he must be the 'Son of Man'. This is Jesus' favourite title for himself. It links with an Old Testament prophecy about a figure who will receive from God a Kingdom that will last forever and will include people of all nations.

Finally, Jesus draws out a deeper lesson from what has happened to the blind man.

*Jesus said, "For judgment I have come into this world, so that the blind will see and those who see will become blind." Some Pharisees who were with him heard him say this and asked, "What? Are we blind too?" Jesus said, "If you were blind, you would not be guilty of sin;*

*but now that you claim you can see, your guilt remains."*

Jesus is saying that people can refuse to see, they can refuse to understand and accept the truth. They choose to be blind.

Jesus claims to be the light of the world. He can enable people to see the truth about themselves, about life and about God.

*

The accounts of Jesus' life speak about him healing the sick, as in this story. They also record occasions when Jesus controls nature, for example when he calms a storm on the Sea of Galilee. He is also said to free people from evil forces and on a few occasions to raise the dead.

These stories have deeper meanings about who Jesus is. For example, he is said to have fed large crowds with small amounts of food. The deeper meaning refers to Jesus satisfying the spiritual hunger in people's hearts. The story of Jesus calming the storm encourages us to find calm and peace within the 'storms' of life by trusting in him.

The miracle stories are telling us that Jesus is unique. There has never been anyone like him. They are claiming that if we put our trust in him and allow him to be part of our lives we will find our spiritual hunger satisfied; we will gain peace in the midst of trouble; we will be freed from destructive forces that drag us down; we will see the truth; we will discover a new quality of life and enter eternal life after we die.

If Jesus did half of the miracles that are attributed to him, he would be unlike anyone else that has ever lived. He would, at the very least, be a prophet from God. He would be truly amazing.

*Lucy*

# Wisdom

**Jesus said ...**

*In everything, do to others what you would have them do to you.*

*My command is this: Love each other as I have loved you. Greater love has no-one than this, that he lay down his life for his friends.*

*Blessed are the merciful. Blessed are the peacemakers.*

*Love your enemies.*

*If someone strikes you on the right cheek, turn to him the other also.*

*Let your 'Yes' be 'Yes' and your 'No', 'No'.*

*This is how you should pray:
'Forgive us our sins as we forgive those who sin against us'.*

*Where your treasure is, there your heart will be also. You cannot serve both God and money.*

*What good is it for someone to gain the whole world, yet forfeit their soul?*

*When you give to the needy,
do not announce it with trumpets,
as the hypocrites do.*

71

*Do not worry ... who of you by worrying can add a single hour to his life?*

*Do not judge. Why do you look at the speck of sawdust in your brother's eye and pay no attention to the plank in your own eye?*

*Enter through the narrow gate. For wide is the gate and broad is the road that leads to destruction.*

*Whoever wants to become great among you must be your servant.*

*The most important commandment is this: 'Love the Lord your God with all your heart and with all your soul and with all your mind and with all your strength.' The second is this: 'Love your neighbour as yourself.'*

*Mollie*

# Identity

There are plenty of people who will try to deceive you by making false claims. There are also people who rightly claim things that are true. And then there are people who deceive themselves.

According to the records of Jesus' life, he made a lot of very striking claims about himself. His favourite way of referring to himself was by using the title 'The Son of Man'. When he did this, and he did it often, he was identifying himself with a prophecy in which the writer sees a vision of someone who is honoured by God and given a Kingdom that lasts forever and includes people from all over the world.

He claimed to have a uniquely close relationship to God and when asked if he was 'The Son of God' he accepted this title too. He said that to know him was to know God and that he was 'the way, the truth and the life.'

He claimed that he had the authority to forgive sins, that one day he would judge the world and that he was the light of the world.

He called himself 'the Lord of the Sabbath', a title which the people of his time would have reserved for God.

He said that he was 'the bread of life' and that he could satisfy people's inner hunger.

These claims are found throughout the accounts of Jesus' life and they leave us with three options:

- We could say that Jesus was deliberately trying to deceive people into thinking he was someone special when he knew it was not true. This would make Jesus a liar who was intentionally out to mislead people.

  The problem is that Jesus insists that people tell the truth. He says that his followers must be so truthful that everyone will know that when they say something they really mean it and can be trusted totally. He himself suffered rejection and execution for the sake of his message.

  Surely, someone who seems to be so committed to truthfulness and is willing to die for their cause would not actually be deliberately lying all along?

- The second possibility is that he was deluded. He thought he was special in the ways that he claimed, but actually he was deceived. On this understanding, Jesus was seriously mentally unstable.

  Jesus however brought teaching to the world that has been admired and cherished for centuries.

Would a mad man attract the interest and attention of so many and be the source of such wisdom?

- The third possibility is that Jesus' claims were perfectly reasonable because they were true. He was simply stating the truth about himself.

I can claim to be the King of a country. I might do this to deceive people in which case I am a bad person. I might do this because I am deluded in which case I am a mad person. However, if I am the King of that country I am simply telling the truth.

# The Flame

Every four years the spectacle of the Olympic Games is staged somewhere in the world. At every location a great torch is lit by a flame that has been carried from the place of the Game's origin in Greece. That flame is passed from person to person and carried by them until finally it reaches its destination.

Down the centuries the story of Jesus has been passed on from generation to generation and from place to place rather like the passing on of that flaming torch. All through those two thousand years, one great event has been the focus of the story that has been told and told again. The very first Christian leaders claimed that they were eye-witnesses of a fact that had dramatically changed their lives. Having seen for themselves and believed, they told their story so that others too could believe and pass the story on. Peter, one of Jesus' contemporaries summed it up like this, *"God has raised this Jesus to life, and we are all witnesses of the fact."*

The story they told and the story that has come down the generations and across the continents is that Jesus, having been publicly executed on a Friday, was miraculously alive again on the following Sunday. And the claim is that this proves that he was no ordinary man and it proves that he has power to give a kind of life that can outlive death itself.

Along a school corridor there are boards with lists of the names of past prize winners. On one of those boards is the name J.N.D.Anderson. He was a pupil of the school and he went on to become Professor of Oriental Laws at London University. He wrote a booklet called "The Evidence for the Resurrection" and he argued that from a legal point of view the claim that Jesus was alive again after his death would stand the test of a court of law.

Firstly, Jesus' tomb was empty. If his body was still around, his enemies would surely have produced it to disprove his followers' claims. And if it was not empty his followers would have made it into a shrine, a place of pilgrimage. So, why was the tomb empty? Who would want to take or move the body? If Jesus followers took the body would they have lived and died for what they knew was a lie?

Secondly, several people claimed that they saw him alive again. Paul, writing in about 55 AD records this list: *"he appeared to Peter, and then to the Twelve. After that, he appeared to more than five hundred of the brothers at the same time, most of whom are still living ... Then he appeared to James, then to all the apostles, and last of all he appeared to me also".*

The details of some of these appearances are found in the accounts of Jesus' life called the Gospels. Another writer says this, *"After his suffering, he showed himself to these men and gave many convincing proofs that he was alive."*

These appearances occurred for a period of time and then stopped. It is also interesting to note that, according to John's Gospel, the first person to see Jesus alive again was a woman. In those days a woman's evidence was valued much less than a man's. It would be very strange, if this was a made up story, for a woman to be chosen as the primary witness.

Thirdly, the Christian Faith burst into the world with dynamic power and spread across the Roman Empire despite outbreaks of cruel persecution. Would this have happened if Jesus had simply been killed and lay dead somewhere in Jerusalem?

And fourthly, Christians down the ages have claimed to relate to a living Jesus not merely a heroic but dead martyr.

These things need explaining - the empty tomb, the appearances, the explosive expansion of Christianity in the Roman world and the on-going experience of Christians of all types, ages and races. Many have found in the resurrection of Jesus a firm foundation for faith, a flaming torch worth carrying and passing on.

Imagine how a detective might investigate the central claim of the Christian Faith:

*Could* God have raised Jesus from the dead?

Surely he could. If he had the power to create the universe he could easily raise Jesus from death.

*Would* God have raised Jesus from the dead?

There are several possible motives that would explain why God would do such a thing. The resurrection could be God's seal of approval on Jesus' death for the sins of the world. It could be a great sign of Jesus' identity as the Son of God. It could be the promise of a life beyond death for those who will follow in Jesus' way.

*Did* God raise Jesus from the dead?

There is compelling evidence: the tomb was empty, Jesus was seen, and his followers were dramatically changed.

## Doubts Dispelled

*"Now Thomas one of the Twelve, was not with the disciples when Jesus came* [i.e. appeared to them after his death]. *So the other disciples told him, 'We have seen the Lord!' But he said to them, 'Unless I see the nail marks in his hands and put my finger where the nails were, and put my hand into his side, I will not believe it.'*

*A week later his disciples were in the house again, and Thomas was with them. Though the doors were locked, Jesus came and stood among them and said, 'Peace be with you!' Then he said to Thomas, 'Put your finger here; see my hands. Reach out your hand and put it into my side. Stop doubting and believe.'*

*Thomas said to him, 'My Lord and my God!'*

*(John chapter 20)*

**So what does it mean?**

**What if Jesus really did defeat death?**

**It would be....**

- a powerful sign telling us that Jesus is like no other person who ever lived.

- a statement of hope. Death does not have the final word. There is life beyond the grave.

- an amazing reversal. The darkness and injustice of Jesus' death are completely turned around. There is no situation that God cannot reverse. Whatever happens, good will triumph in the end.

- a clear confirmation that God accepted Jesus' death for the sins of the world.

# The Key

There are a lot of things that prove friendship. A true friend will listen to you; a true friend will spend time with you; they will travel distances in order to see you.

Imagine you are living in a war zone. Shells explode near to your house every day and night. Food is in short supply, water has to be rationed and the electricity is down. Disease is rampant. Imagine a friend who travels from a safe place to be alongside you in such circumstances. That would be a true friend indeed.

Jesus is that kind of friend. He has shared in our human experience. He suffered injustice, cruelty and death; he experienced the dark side of humanity. Why? He did it because he is a true friend who shares our experiences, even the experience of death itself.

But when we think about Jesus' death we discover an even deeper meaning.

Jewish people have a special day called the Day of Atonement. Long ago this day involved certain rituals. A goat was chosen and a priest put his hands on it and as he rested his hands on the animal, he confessed the people's sins, the moral failure in their lives. He spoke about how they had not loved God with all their heart, how they had not loved other people properly and how they had done and said and thought things that were not acceptable to God. And then when the priest had finished, the goat was sent off into the wilderness. The chosen goat acted as a scapegoat. It was as if it had taken the people's sins on itself and carried them away.

Christians understand Jesus to have voluntarily offered himself as the final scapegoat. When he died on the cross he took on himself the fearful opposition of God towards all the evil in the world.

God is truly and totally good. He cannot just overlook things that are wrong. Jesus voluntarily took on himself the guilt of the human race. He carried our moral failings. Jesus took the blame and the punishment for us.

*"We all, like sheep, have gone astray, each of us has turned to his own way; and the LORD has laid on him the iniquity of us all."* (The Prophet Isaiah)

The name 'Jesus' means rescuer or saviour and the Christmas story states that he will be called 'Jesus' because he will rescue people from their sins.

His death is the great act of atonement. Through his death we can be at-one with God; we can be reconciled with God. Putting our trust in what Jesus has done for us is the key that opens the door to a friendship with God, now and forever.

# The Rescue

The following took place in the USA. It is the story of nine coal miners who were working about eighty metres underground south east of Pittsburgh in Pennsylvania.

**This is what happened:**

*It was a Wednesday and they thought they were digging about a hundred metres away from some old abandoned workings, but actually their map was wrong and they were dangerously close to millions of gallons of water that had collected in a chamber that had not been worked for fifty years.*

*As they cut through the rock they unleashed a torrent and the mine that they had been working in was flooded. Somehow the nine miners managed to take refuge in a small chamber that acted as an air pocket. There they sat, huddled together trying to keep each other warm. They had a serious problem. They were trapped 80 metres below ground and there was no way out. They decided to rope themselves together so that if they drowned, any 'rescuers' would find all of the bodies. They wrote notes to their loved ones and put them together in a bucket. They could do nothing to save themselves.*

*But up above a rescue plan was underway. On Thursday afternoon a huge drill arrived. The plan was to create a shaft large enough to lower a large bucket which the trapped miners could climb into and then be pulled up to the surface. By Friday morning the drill had reached to within 8 metres of the chamber where the nine miners were huddled together. And then disaster. The drill bit broke and fell into the hole so that the rescuers had to abandon the shaft. But those above ground were not going to give up. They valued and loved those miners and they were going to do everything they could to save them.*

*At 10.30 on Saturday morning they started to drill a second escape shaft and finally on Saturday night having worked since Wednesday they broke through. They lowered down a phone and imagine how they felt when they discovered that all nine were still alive.*

*And so it was that early on Sunday morning after a total of about 77 hours the nine miners were brought to the surface one by one. And when the last one was finally rescued the celebrations could begin. "All nine! All nine!" shouted the Governor of Pennsylvania as he pumped his fist into the air.*

Every effort was made to save those nine miners and when they were rescued they knew how much they were valued and loved. Of course they had to respond to their rescuers. They could have chosen to stay where they were and refused the offer of rescue, but surely no-one would be that foolish, would they?

## Twenty Facts

- It looks like there is a world out there.
- Some things are alive and are made up of organised systems that work.
- We exist and we can experience, think about and respond to the world around us.
- There is beauty and goodness in the world but there is suffering and evil too.

- People make judgements about right and wrong.
- People believe in truth, justice and love.
- The same person can do good and bad things.
- Good people and bad people suffer.
- We will all die one day.
- A lot of stories are about a struggle between good and evil with good winning in the end.
- A lot of human beings take faith and spirituality seriously.
- Many people claim to experience the presence of God.
- Religion has inspired good things and evil things.

- There are stories about a man called Jesus that have been written down, valued and passed on through many centuries.
- There are stories about Jesus doing miracles.
- There are stories about Jesus dying and then being alive again.
- The teaching of Jesus is still read, studied and admired.
- All kinds of people claim to have a friendship with God through Jesus.
- Millions of people worship Jesus as Lord and God.
- Many people have been willing to suffer rather than deny their faith.

# What if ...

... there is an eternal mind that exists beyond time and caused the universe to exist?

... there is an intelligence that caused the universe to follow mathematical laws and to have just the right conditions for life to evolve?

... there is an eternal being who wanted there to be free and intelligent creatures who could know him?

... this being was good, creative and loving and wanted there to be creatures who could be like this too?

... this Mind loved people and so entered their world as one of them?

What if there is a God? That would explain a lot.

*What do you see?*

**GODISNOWHERE**

# Questions

(god) efficient cause sculptor

(no) material cause —
blocks of sculpt

NO PRE-EXISTING MATERIAL
↓
rejects
Metaphysical
dualism

# Suffering

Crucifixion was a horrible way to die. The Romans reserved it, as a means of execution, for common criminals and it was not spoken of in polite society.

It has often been pointed out that a cross is a strange sign for a religious movement to adopt. Imagine wearing a miniature electric chair around your neck; imagine an electric chair hanging from the walls of a place where people meet, or stamped onto the front of a songbook in order to inspire the singers. Everyone would be offended at such an idea and yet the cross, the sign of the Christian faith, represents perhaps the cruellest means of execution ever invented. Jesus, like many other victims, was nailed through the wrists and ankles and left to die of suffocation or heart failure.

It is the death of Jesus on a Roman cross that marks out the Christian faith from all other faiths. The bold claim is that in the person of Jesus, God has visited our world as a human being and suffered death at the hands of his own creatures. Christians believe in a God of power, a God who made and holds together the universe, but the Christian God is also one who has become a man and suffered hatred, injustice and pain. No other religion has a suffering God like this.

The existence of suffering, is however, a reason that some give for rejecting the Christian faith. If God is powerful and loving, why does he not do something about the suffering in the world? Either he is not powerful enough to do anything about it or he does not care enough to bother. A God of such limited power is not worth worshipping and a God who does not love is no better than us.

Part of an answer to this objection is that we know that God cares, because of Jesus. God cares enough to come alongside us and to experience the injustice and the evil of this world. God is our friend. In Jesus he has visited us and cared for those in need and in Jesus' suffering and death he has shown that he does not keep his distance from the realities that so many face in their lives.

This is not a complete answer, but it is part of an answer. God has not sat in heaven with his feet up and left us to it, he knows what we go through and he feels it too.

There is of course more that we can say in response to the problem of suffering. There is what is called 'The Free Will Defence'. It goes something like this: imagine you have a friend whose friendship you really value. Then one day you discover that they had not chosen to be your friend, rather they had been forced into it. The friendship would suddenly be meaningless. Friendship has to be chosen to be real. Love cannot be programmed. A robot cannot be a true friend. The only way that a relationship can be meaningful and real is if it is chosen and for a relationship to be chosen there has to be the possibility of not choosing it.

It is the same with goodness. An action that is programmed cannot be praised as good or punished as bad; it is simply what the robot had to do.

If friendship with God and with others is the reason for us being here, God had to make creatures that could choose to be friends or choose not to be. If doing the good thing matters then there has to be the real possibility of choosing not to do it. That is who we are, creatures that can choose and creatures whose choices matter. Sadly much of the suffering in the world results from people choosing to cause harm. The only alternative is to take the choice away, then no-one could cause suffering but doing the right thing would not mean anything anymore either.

I suppose God could have decided not to make us at all because of all the trouble we would cause, but that would mean that ultimately evil controls the universe. God's hands would have been tied by the knowledge that we would choose to do wrong.

There is still more that we could say. Imagine you could design a universe. What sort of universe would you make? Is any kind of universe possible? Even God cannot make a round square or an irresistible force that will collide with an immovable object.

Could God make a world with no suffering or pain and would that be the best possible world? It is certainly true that *some* suffering can make us deeper, more mature people and *some* pain is useful; ask someone who has lost the ability to feel pain!

Darwin's ideas might help us here. He suggests that it is only through struggle that nature, life and consciousness emerge. Perhaps the amazing diversity and beauty of living things is only possible in a world shaped by suffering.

These answers are important, but suffering is not just a philosophical issue, it is much more painful and personal than that. Personal suffering or the suffering of someone close to us can push our trust in God to the very edge of unbelief and can even drive us over the edge.

When someone we love is struggling with cancer or our baby dies, we are faced with a very painful choice. We can reject God and say 'I cannot understand this, I cannot accept this, I do not believe.' Or we can make a different choice and say, 'I cannot understand this, but I am willing to trust. I will trust God.'

Personal suffering brings us to a very challenging and difficult crossroads; in one direction is the way of rejection, in the other direction the way of trust. It is a painful but vital choice. Rejection can lead to a hard heart, trust brings strength with which to face the hard times.

We are small creatures on a small planet in a big universe. It is reasonable to accept that some things are beyond our understanding; sometimes the reasonable but difficult thing is to accept the mystery and trust.

There is another thing that is also hard for us to grasp. We only see part of the picture. For us, personal suffering or the suffering of a loved one can seem to be too much. It can go on for too long and be too terrible.

It is possible however, that one day the suffering will look different when we are able to see it in the light of eternity. If there is a life beyond this life, the struggles that we go through now will one day take on a very different proportion and perspective.

The Apostle Paul knew something about suffering in his own life and he could write: *"I consider that our present sufferings are not worth comparing with the glory that will be revealed in us."* As a Christian he could say: *"I am convinced that neither death nor life, neither angels nor demons, neither the present nor the future ... nor anything else in all creation, will be able to separate us from the love of God that is in Christ Jesus our Lord."*

Jesus' suffering and death were very terrible for him and for his family and friends, but the story does not end there. The darkness of death gave way to life and to hope. There truly was a light at the end of the tunnel. The resurrection of Jesus gives a reason for optimism despite the anguish and suffering in the world.

The writer of the final book of the Bible says this: *Then I saw a new heaven and a new earth ... He (God) will wipe every tear from their eyes. There will be no more death or mourning or crying or pain, for the old order of things has passed away."*

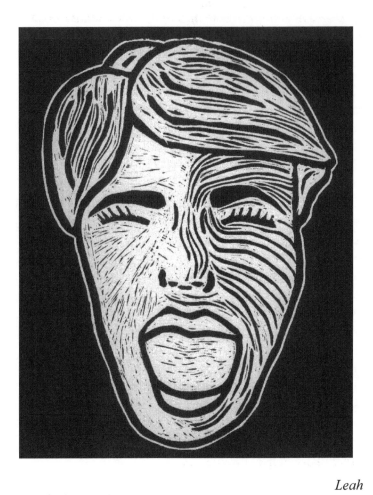

*Leah*

# At the End of Time

*At the end of time, billions of people were seated on a great plain before God's throne. Most shrank back from the brilliant light before them, but some talked heatedly.*

*"How can God judge us?" snapped a young woman. She ripped open a sleeve to reveal a tattooed number from a Nazi concentration camp. "We endured terror ... beatings ... torture ... death!"*

*In another group a man lowered his collar. "What about this?" he demanded, showing an ugly rope burn. "Lynched, for no crime but being black!" In another crowd there was a pregnant schoolgirl with sullen eyes: "Why should I suffer?" she murmured. "It wasn't my fault."*

*Far out across the plain were hundreds of such groups. Each had a complaint against God for the evil and suffering he had permitted in his world. How lucky God was to live in Heaven, where all was sweetness and light and where there was no weeping or fear, no hunger or hatred. What did God know of all that human beings have to endure in this world? "God leads a pretty sheltered life", they said.*

*So each of these groups sent forward their leader, chosen because he had suffered the most. In the centre of the vast plain, they consulted with each other. At last they were ready to present their case. Before God could be qualified to be their judge, he must endure what they had endured. Their decision was that God should be sentenced to live on earth as a man.*

*Let the legitimacy of his birth be doubted. Give him a work so difficult that even his family will think him out of his mind. Let him be betrayed by his closest friends. Let him face false charges, be tried by a prejudiced jury and convicted by a cowardly judge. Let him be tortured. At the last, let him see what it means to be terribly alone. Then let him die.*

*As each leader announced their case, loud murmurs of approval went up from the assembled throng of people.*

*When the last had finished pronouncing sentence, there was a long silence. No one uttered a word. No one moved, for suddenly, they all knew that God had already served his sentence.*

*(Adapted. Original author unknown)*

# Silence

Why does God not make himself more obvious? Why does God seem silent and hidden? Perhaps this story helps:

*There was once a young, handsome and powerful King. The unmarried women in the noble families of the land wondered which one of them would become his Queen.*

*One day the King was riding back to his palace. On passing through a small village he noticed a young peasant woman working in the field beside the road and something about her attracted his attention. He did not mention this to anyone, but he just could not stop thinking about her. The next time he was riding that way he deliberately slowed his horse so that he could look for her and there she was again.*

*The King summoned his most trusted adviser and told him about the girl and his feelings for her, but unsurprisingly the advice he received was not what he wanted to hear: 'Your majesty would be wise to put her out of mind. There are many beautiful young women of noble birth who would be glad to be your Queen'. The King knew that his adviser was wise and sensible but he had come to love the peasant girl despite her lowly situation. Each time he saw her, as he passed through her village, his love grew until he longed to talk to her and tell her of his feelings for her.*

*He culled his adviser again and announced that he wished to marry the peasant girl and make her his*

*Queen. The adviser seeing that the King was determined replied, 'If your majesty insists, then I will have her brought here to you'.*

*The King, however, knew that if the girl was brought into his palace and saw him in all his splendour, she would bow before him and submit to whatever he commanded. He knew that she would obey and become his Queen, but he wanted her love not merely her obedience. The royal adviser offered a solution: 'What if you visited her in her own village and proposed to her there?' The King knew however, that she and her parents would be overpowered by his presence. They would simply bow down and do his bidding. 'No', said the King, 'she must not know who I am. I will enter her world and live and work in her village. I will dress and eat and live as a peasant lives. I will try to win her love and only then will she discover that I am her King'. 'But what if she doesn't return your love?' someone asked. 'That is a risk I have to take', replied the King.*

*And so in the name of love, the King left his palace. He put aside his majesty, his power and his wealth. He dressed and lived and worked in that other world. And each morning he awoke hoping with all his heart that the peasant girl would love him in return and then one day become his Queen.*

*(Inspired by Søren Kierkegaard)*

# Miracles

Towards the end of his account of the life of Jesus, John says this: *"Jesus did many other miraculous signs in the presence of his disciples, which are not recorded in this book. But these are written that you may believe that Jesus is the Christ, the Son of God, and that by believing you may have life in his name."*

For John, the miracles of Jesus were signs that Jesus was someone we should put our trust in. John focuses on seven such signs: three involve healing people – a blind man, a disabled person and someone with a fever; three further stories show Jesus exercising power over nature – walking on water, feeding a large crowd with a small amount of food and turning water into wine at a wedding; and the remaining miracle brought a man back from death and points forward to the great sign of Jesus' own resurrection.

When we travel we look for signs to point us in the direction of our destination. We do not stop at the sign itself. The sign shows us the way to what we are really looking for. The miracles of Jesus, according to John, are similar. They help us to discover who Jesus is and they encourage us to put our trust in him. Miracles are signs that carry a message, they are not magic tricks that merely surprise and entertain.

For John, the miracles of Jesus provided convincing evidence that would help people to believe. For millions of people down the centuries and for many people today the miracles of Jesus have been and are a powerful reason for listening to his teaching and claims, trusting him and trying to follow his way in their lives.

For other people though, miracles create problems rather than being a positive reason to believe. We might ask the following questions:

- 'Can miracles happen; surely science has shown us that the laws of nature are fixed?'
- 'Why did miracles happen in Bible times but not today?'
- 'Didn't people in the past believe in supernatural events in a way that we don't today?'
- 'Isn't the weight of evidence always against miracles?'
- 'If God can do miracles why doesn't he do more of them to help sick and suffering people?'
- 'Different religions claim miracles so don't they cancel each other out?'

- **Can miracles happen; surely science has shown us that the laws of nature are fixed?**

A miracle is sometimes said to be an event which breaks the laws of nature, but this may not be very helpful.

If I drop an object, the 'law' of gravity says that it will fall to the ground and experience teaches that this happens again and again. If, however, I introduce another factor, for example I put my hand under the object and move my arm upwards, then things go differently. The object rises as I lift it up. It is not that the 'law' of gravity has been broken but that due to some other factor things have happened differently this time.

In a similar way it is quite reasonable to believe that God has created a world that behaves according to certain 'laws'. The world is predictable, things normally happen in the same way and so scientists can work out the 'laws' of nature. If, however, there is a God who is powerful enough to create the universe he could cause things to happen differently sometimes.

- **Why did miracles happen in Bible times but not today?**

You may have come across a 'town crier' somewhere. He is dressed in old-fashioned clothes, he has a hand-bell that he rings and he shouts, 'Hear ye! Hear ye!' before delivering his message. He makes a noise to get you to listen.

A miracle might be defined as an amazing event caused by a supernatural power. Miracles are therefore bound to be rare. If miracles happened often they would no longer be amazing, but part of everyday life. And so it is that miracles are rare even in the Bible. The Bible story covers a period of many hundreds of years and miracles are clustered around three points in time. Miracles happen at the time of Moses (the great liberator and law giver), at the time of Elijah and Elisha (great prophets) and at the time of Jesus (the great saviour, prophet and teacher) and his apostles.

It would seem that the miracles in the Bible are a bit like the town crier's bell, they are signs saying, 'Listen!' It is as if God is saying, 'Listen to Moses and his laws'; 'Listen to the prophets and their message'; 'Listen to Jesus and his apostles'.

Miracles are bound to be rare and in the Bible they seem to act as a kind of wakeup call telling people that something unusually significant is taking place.

This is not to say that miracles never happened at other times in the Bible story or that they can never happen today, but rather that we should not expect miracles to happen very often.

- **Didn't people in the past believe in supernatural events in a way that we don't today?**

People in Bible times believed that the universe is an open, rather than a closed, system. That is, they believed in God as a supernatural spiritual power who could make things happen in our physical universe. They knew that blind people did not usually suddenly regain their sight, they knew that dead people stay dead and that a small amount of food does not satisfy five thousand people. In Mark's account of Jesus' life he says that people were 'amazed' by what Jesus did. And John clearly thought that the signs he related would help people to believe that Jesus was unlike anyone else because Jesus did things that no-one else could do.

Some people today believe that our physical universe is a closed system and that there is no supernatural power that can act into our world. If this is true then genuine miracles cannot happen and such claims would need to be explained in some other way.

Clearly people in Bible times did see the world differently to the way some people see it today. The question is, were they right to see the universe as an open system or should we all see it as closed?

There is a basic difference of belief here. Some believe that the universe is closed; some believe that it is open.

However, the situation is not quite that simple. There are those who believe in God and in Jesus but question belief in miracles. They suggest that the miracle accounts are stories with a meaning, they are 'myths' designed to teach us important things about Jesus and his mission. For example, the account of Jesus healing a blind man is about Jesus opening people's eyes to the truth rather than a description of Jesus actually physically healing someone.

This approach removes miracles as a problem, but it could be said to raise as many questions as it answers. The New Testament writers themselves do not seem to see their writings in this way. Here are some of the things that they say:

One writer talks about information *"handed down to us by ... eye-witnesses..."*

Another says, *"We did not follow cleverly invented stories when we told you about the power and coming of our Lord Jesus Christ, but we were eye-witnesses of his majesty."*

And another: *"We proclaim to you what we have seen and heard."*

We might also ask why people would come to believe that Jesus was so special if he did not actually do these special things.

Some people suggest a different way of approaching Jesus' miracles. They say that he did not use supernatural power but rather he had exceptional skills. He was such a charismatic figure that he could inspire a crowd of five thousand to share their food so that all had enough. He could give a crippled person the courage and confidence to overcome their problem and walk. On this view Jesus did do extraordinary things, but by means of his unique qualities of mind and personality.

While such an idea might be used to explain some of the miracles of Jesus it is difficult to see how it could account for all of them, especially the most important miracle of them all - Jesus' own resurrection.

This is not a simple issue but it does seem reasonable to say that if God was present in the world in the life of

Jesus in a one-off, special way, then it would not be surprising if Jesus' life was accompanied by amazing signs.

- **Isn't the weight of evidence always against miracles?**

A well-known argument against believing in miracles works like this: the evidence that dead people stay dead, for example, runs into millions upon millions of cases. How many people do you know who were dead once and are now alive? None, of course!

So, however strong the evidence is for one man (Jesus) dying and then being alive again, it is never strong enough to outweigh the massive evidence on the other side. Add to this that eye-witnesses are often unreliable and that people love unusual stories and it is clearly not reasonable to believe that Jesus died and rose again.

There is logic to this argument, but there is a problem with it too. Supposing Jesus died and then was seen alive again. According to this argument we would be wrong to believe it even though it really happened. It would leave us unable to believe the truth. It might be a clever argument, but it may not lead us to the truth and surely the truth is what matters most.

And eye-witnesses can be reliable, in fact our law courts use their evidence all of the time.

And the argument that ordinary people who die stay dead, does not apply if Jesus was not an ordinary person.

- **If God can do miracles why doesn't he do more of them to help sick and suffering people?**

This question can be put very bluntly in both personal and global terms. If Jesus cured a blind man why does he not cure the person I love who suffers terribly and then dies from cancer? If Jesus could feed a crowd of five thousand why does he let hundreds of thousands of people go hungry in the world today?

Part of a response to this is found in 'the free-will defence'. If God is to respect our human freedom and allow us to be more significant than robots he cannot keep on interfering in the world. He must allow us to take responsibility and leave us to choose whether we do things that help or harm others. We have to take responsibility and stop harming others and start solving the problems.

Imagine a thirty-year-old man whose mother always stepped in to change things whenever he made wrong decisions. Such a person would never grow up and would be pitied by others. God allows us, individually and as a human race, to grow up and to be independent human beings. We have the gift of freedom, which makes life worthwhile, but we can also abuse that freedom in ways that cause others to suffer.

Perhaps this also applies to the natural world. God allows the world the freedom to function according to its natural processes. If God were to repeatedly interfere with the world there could be all sorts of knock on effects. We know how an ecosystem consists of many inter-related organisms. To take action on behalf of one of these might have unforeseen effects on the whole system. A miracle to change the weather conditions for the better in one place might have disastrous effects somewhere else. A miracle done for one person might have negative consequences for hundreds of other people later on. This is similar to the so called 'Butterfly Effect'. A small change in one place can multiply and have a big knock on effect elsewhere.

We might therefore expect God to intervene in the world as little as possible so as to allow us to become mature people who live in a world that is delicately balanced and behaves predictably according to scientific 'laws'. It might be very difficult to live in a world that was unpredictable because God kept on interfering.

It is reasonable to believe in a God who has performed miracles, for particular reasons, at key moments in human history. Such a God could choose to intervene again and may sometimes respond to people's prayers in surprising ways, but generally the world behaves in a more straightforward, balanced and predictable way and we are allowed the freedom to act in ways that can benefit or harm others.

In the end a realistic humility might also lead us to say that God knows best how to run the world and when and where to intervene. He knows best when to say 'yes' and when to say 'no' or 'not yet' to our prayers. Given our smallness and his greatness there are bound to be things that remain a mystery, things that are beyond the limits of our knowledge and understanding.

- **Different religions claim miracles so don't they cancel each other out?**

The issue here is that if Christian miracles are said to show that Christianity is true and other religions also claim to be true on the basis of their own miracles, we end up with different faiths contradicting each other so that their miracle claims become useless.

There are however two other possible approaches.

> 1. *We could compare the miracle stories of different religions and then choose the religion whose miracle claims are most convincing.*

Some miracles might be more compelling than others:

- Real miracles will carry important meanings rather than being merely magical. Legends tend to be elaborate with plenty of fanciful details. One of the striking things about the miracles of Jesus in the Bible is how understated they are.

- We might also look at how a claimed miracle fits into a set of beliefs. Is it just a bizarre or sensational story or does it make sense as part of a bigger framework?

- And then there is the question of sources. We can ask who wrote the story and when. This can help us to decide how seriously to take a particular account.

- We could also consider the possibility that a particular 'miracle' could come from a deceptive, rather than a good, supernatural origin. Counterfeit miracles are a possibility.

By applying these kinds of criteria we can compare the miracle claims of different traditions and this might lead us to believe one and not another.

> 2. *If we were to find that specific miracles from different faiths are equally compelling, we could take them to be signs of spiritual truth within these different traditions, rather than seeing them as cancelling one another out. Different religions would, in this respect, be seen as complimentary rather than contradictory.*

Finally, it would seem that when we compare religions, Jesus proves to be unique in the history of the world. He is said to have performed many miracles and these are full of meaning and fit into a coherent framework of beliefs. They are reported in a down to earth way and were written down not long after the events. His miracles are clearly from a good source as they are full of compassion and kindness.

In terms of miracles, no other figure in the history of the world's religions compares to Jesus.

# Science

It is not easy to put ourselves in the shoes of people who lived long ago so that we see the world through their eyes. Can you imagine being alive in 1861 when an exhibition of stuffed gorillas took place in London? Very few Europeans had ever seen a gorilla. Crowds flocked to see the exhibition and the Daily Telegraph expressed concern that the idea that humans might be related to these creatures could 'have disastrous consequences to the national peace'! On hearing such an idea the Bishop of Worcester's wife is reported to have exclaimed: *'Descended from apes! My dear, let us hope it is not so; but if it is, that it does not become generally known.'*

A difficult shift in self-understanding was going on in the second half of the nineteenth century.

In 1859 Charles Darwin published 'The Origin of Species' and later another book called 'The Descent of Man'. The ideas contained in these volumes have been hard for some to swallow. They suggest that human beings are the result of a long process of evolution and that our ancestors were ape-like creatures.

This was not however the first time that people had to make a dramatic shift in the way they saw themselves. As we have seen already, people once thought that the earth was at the centre of the universe with all of the stars and planets circling around us. Copernicus, Galileo and others put pay to such an idea and people had to adjust to the view that the sun, not the earth, was at the centre of our solar system. We now know that we live in one of the many, many galaxies of a vast universe.

Our understanding of the earth and ourselves has dramatically changed and some suggest that these scientific advances also push the idea of a Creator out of the picture. They suggest that the creation story of Genesis is redundant now that Darwin has shown us a better way, although Darwin himself said, *"I see no reason why the views given in this volume [The Origin of Species] should offend the religious feelings of any one."*

These issues are hugely important to us as human beings because they raise big questions about our identity and significance. Do we have any special importance in this huge universe?

Firstly, we ought to say that there are many scientists who believe in God, so perhaps these questions can be answered in a way that is friendly to faith.

Science itself depends on the world behaving in a rational, predictable and law abiding way. We could not do science if the world was not like this. Belief in a rational Creator explains why the universe has these characteristics. Nature is not random or magical because it is the creation of a rational mind and many scientists have seen their scientific research as 'thinking God's thoughts after him.'

We could add that if there is an infinitely powerful Creator, we should not be surprised if the universe is unimaginably vast and that our planet is not at the centre of everything. We have no idea how many planets with intelligent life a Creator might choose to make.

But what about Genesis and Adam and Eve and all that? There are lots of things that could be said here, but let us start with this:

What makes a story a true story? Take Jesus' famous parable of the Good Samaritan. It is a story about someone who was beaten up and robbed. Some passers-by ignore him, but someone of a different race and religion stops to help. Many people believe this to be a true story; it is true that we should help people in need regardless of their race or religion. The people who passed by on the other side were wrong. The stranger who stopped to help was right. Jesus told this story to teach something true and important.

Perhaps the creation stories in Genesis are true in the same kind of way, not because they are a scientific description, but because they teach the truth about there being a God who made us, the world and the whole universe.

The story of Adam and Eve taking the fruit, having been tempted by the snake, can be seen as a parable of human nature that describes our attitude to God and to temptation. It is a story of how things could have been if it were not for human sin.

Adam and Eve could also have been real Middle-Eastern, Neolithic people who rebelled against God. To report this in a factual way would however make a rather boring, easily forgotten account, so it has been passed on in a more imaginative and memorable story.

The point is that a story can be powerful and can teach us true things without it having to be a straightforward and literal description of events.

When it comes to the Theory of Evolution there is no reason why God should not use a long process of evolution to create life on earth. Creating something slowly is no less wonderful than creating it instantly. You can make instant coffee or filter coffee but the quicker method is not necessarily the better method.

At the end of 'The Origin of Species', Darwin said this, *"There is grandeur in this view of life, with its several powers, having been originally breathed by the Creator into a few forms or into one; and that whilst this planet has gone cycling on according to the fixed law of gravity, from so simple a beginning endless forms most beautiful and most wonderful have been, and are being evolved."*

One mistake people make is to think that there have to be gaps in our scientific knowledge in order to make room for God. In this view, God is called in to explain what science does not understand. This has an obvious outcome in that the more we discover, the less room there will be for God until he becomes completely unnecessary. This so-called 'God of the Gaps' approach would rightly give God a limited life expectancy, but God is the creator of and the explanation for the whole of nature not just the bits we do not yet understand.

There is no gap in a Shakespeare play that the existence of Shakespeare explains. Shakespeare is the explanation of the whole play. In the same way we should not expect to find gaps in our scientific understanding that we then explain by the existence of God. God is the author of the whole story.

Imagine one day a letter arrives in the post for you. You open the envelope to find a piece of paper in the middle of which is drawn a red heart. To the top left is the letter 'I' and in the bottom right is the letter 'U'. Science, you believe, gives all of the answers to life's questions. So you take the piece of paper to a laboratory and ask one of the scientists to analyse it for you. At the end of the day you fetch the results. You now know the dimensions of the piece of paper and its weight. You know what the paper is made of and what chemicals the ink consists of. In scientific terms you have a complete explanation of the piece of paper that dropped through your door. You could say that the piece of paper is 'nothing but'… and then you could list all of the scientific data.

No one would ever do this of course. Everyone knows that as well as the physical explanation, the piece of paper has another more important explanation. There is a personal explanation in terms of who sent it and why. There does not need to be a gap in the scientific explanation for the personal bit to fit into. The physical and personal explanations are different kinds of explanation that can both be true.

Science does a great job at telling us what things are made of and how they work. It is brilliant at answering physical questions. There are, though, other kinds of questions that are also vitally important. Personal questions like who, if anybody, made the universe? And why did they do it? Religious stories and teachings are trying to answer those kinds of questions. Science can do great things but it cannot tell us whether or not someone made us and cares for us.

And science cannot tell us the right or wrong way to live. It can tell us how to make a bomb, but it cannot tell us whether it is ever right to use a bomb against other people. Moral questions are not scientific questions; they depend on what we value and what we believe about human beings, about the world and about God.

We need both religion and science if we are to find the answers that we need and if we are to live life to the full.

Current scientific theories tell us of a 'Big Bang' that gave rise to the universe and a long process of evolution by means of natural selection that gave rise to life on earth, but these theories raise the biggest question of them all. Why is there a universe, and why does the universe function in a rational way and why did life on earth evolve? God is the big answer to these big questions. God is not a kind of poly-filler to fill the cracks in our knowledge. God is the reason why we and the universe are here at all.

It is probably true to say that we are more aware of the power and also of the limitations of science than any previous generation. We can see its power in the benefits of technology and medicine. We live in exciting times when things are possible that people in the past would have considered unbelievable.

The limitations of science are however also very evident. Science can give us the ability to create weapons of terrifying destruction and it can give us power over the very stuff of life itself. It cannot however, tell us what we should or should not do, it cannot tell us how we should live. Science needs a framework of beliefs and values to guide it. Left to itself, science could turn out to be a monster that will destroy us, rather than a tool for our good.

---

**Atheism – a problem:**

If our minds are the product of physical processes alone and the aim of those processes is the survival of our genes, why should we trust our minds to lead us to the truth?

Will our minds not simply be adapted to lead us to what best enables us to survive and to reproduce, regardless of the truth?

---

# Religions

3x3=9.

There is a right answer and lots of possible wrong answers. Nine is right; ten, eight and eleven are all wrong. Are the different religions of the world like the answers to a maths problem? Has one religion got the right answers and the others the wrong answers? Or are they all right in some ways and wrong in others?

Languages are different to sums.

The same thing can be said in different languages. You can tell someone who you are in French, Russian and Arabic. What you say will sound different and if you write it down it will look different, but it is the same thing just expressed in different ways. Are the religions of the world like different languages, all saying the same things but in their own way?

The languages model would seem to be true in some ways. Islam and Christianity for example, both tell us that there is more to life than the material; that there is a God; that God is our judge; that God is merciful and compassionate; that we should help the poor; that prayer is important and that there is a life after death. In the Koran and the Bible, Islam and Christianity seem to be saying the same things in their own ways. There is plenty of common ground.

Honesty requires us however, to face the fact that there are also important differences.

At the heart of the Christian faith is the crucifixion and resurrection of Jesus. Muslims do not believe that Jesus was crucified. For Muslims, Jesus is a Prophet and the Messiah and therefore God would not have let him be executed by the Romans as if he were a common criminal. Jesus did not die at the hands of the Romans and he did not rise again.

Christians believe that Jesus was executed on a Friday but later that weekend he was seen alive again.

There is clearly an important point of difference here. It is either true that Jesus was crucified and rose again or it is not. This sounds more like two different answers to a maths problem. They cannot both be right.

This has important implications and leads to different answers to the question of how we can be on good terms with God. The Christian faith says that when Jesus died he offered himself as a sacrifice for human sin.

According to Islam, Jesus is a prophet, for Christians he is both a prophet and a saviour.

This difference goes even deeper. Christians see in the suffering of Jesus something very important about God. In Jesus' death, God allows himself to be weak and vulnerable. He is a God of power who made the universe, but he is also a God who shares in human suffering and works through weakness and what appears like failure. In Islam, God is powerful not vulnerable. In Christianity, God is powerful but he also shares in our weakness.

Christians and Muslims have much in common but there are also important differences. In some ways they are saying the same things in different 'languages'; in other ways they are giving different answers to the same 'sums'.

However, the fact that Islam and Christianity are different does not mean that there needs to be hostility and hatred between them.

Jesus called people to love others regardless of race or religion. For Christians the decisive event in the history of the world is Jesus' selfless death and surprising resurrection. Jesus' willingness to die was a rejection of self-asserting violence whether this is carried out in the name of Christianity, Islam or anything else. Jesus' death was a commitment to self-denial and love. Christians are therefore called to a life of love which leaves no room for hatred of others on religious or any other grounds.

If Jesus conquered death then he is the one above all others that we should listen to and it is Jesus himself who says, *"I am the way and the truth and the life. No-one comes to the Father except through me."*

So does this mean that only Christians will get to heaven? The Christian faith claims that the way we get to heaven is by having our sins forgiven through Jesus' death for us. Those who experience God's love in this way are changed and want to respond by living in a way that pleases God.

God is our judge and he will judge everyone fairly. We will all face the God of love and justice. A loving and fair God would not reject people just because they have never heard of Jesus. All who recognize their own shortcomings and seek God's mercy will be forgiven and welcomed into heaven. Their sins will be forgiven because Jesus died for them and this will be true for people who have heard of Jesus and have responded to him by name, as well as for all who have been genuinely humble before God.

In the last book of his Chronicles of Narnia, C S Lewis describes a scene in which the lion, Aslan, stands beside a great doorway. All of the creatures approach him and there is a moment of judgement. Those who can look Aslan in the face, with love, go in through the door and on to a new adventure. Those who do not love him turn away and take a different path.

Jesus described two people at the Temple:

*Two people went to pray.*

*One stood up and prayed,*
*'God, I thank you that I believe the right things and*
*worship in the right way.'*
*The other bowed to the ground and said,*
*'God, have mercy on me, a sinner.'*

*Which one, do you think, went away accepted by God?*

\*\*\*

*Tvesa*

## Health Warning: Religion can be bad for you

Science and technology can be used to enrich our lives but they can also be misused in destructive and negative ways. They give us medicines to cure but also weapons to kill. Sharp knives can save lives through surgery but they can also take lives through murder.

Religion is the same. It can be used to enrich people's lives and it can be used to distort, limit and control.

Jesus was very critical of the religious leaders of his day. Bad religion in his view:

- burdens, condemns and excludes people.
- focuses on small rules while neglecting the bigger issues.
- encourages religious people to feel morally and spiritually superior.
- is marked by hypocrisy – pretending to be something you are not really.
- is preoccupied with appearances, status, titles and man-made traditions.

Jesus said that true and false religion can be recognised by what they produce in people's lives, they are known by their 'fruit'. True religion shapes your character in a positive way. It is not so much about what you say you believe, but rather how your beliefs change the things you do and the kind of person you become. The Apostle Paul said that when God is really present in a person's life they gradually become more loving, joyful, peaceful, patient, kind, good, faithful, gentle and self-controlled.

For Jesus, generosity and forgiveness are key signs of real faith. True religion is to love God with your whole heart and to love others whoever they are.

In his letter to an early Christian community Paul writes that love is the mark of genuine religion and any religious activity that lacks love is worthless:

*"If I have the gift of prophecy and can fathom all mysteries and all knowledge, and if I have a faith that can move mountains, but have not love, I am nothing. If I give all I possess to the poor and surrender my body to the flames, but have not love, I gain nothing."*

History proves that religion, like science and most other things, can be used for good and for evil. It would be foolish to reject something that has such potential for good just because some people use it badly.

An enormous amount of good has been done in the name of religion. Imagine a world without William Wilberforce, Lord Shaftesbury, William Booth, Thomas Barnardo, George Cadbury, Elizabeth Fry, Mother Teresa, Martin Luther King, Desmond Tutu and countless others.

## Violence in the Bible

The first half of the Bible includes some grim tales. A famous example is the battle for the city of Jericho. The Israelites had escaped from slavery in Egypt and entered the land of Canaan which they intended to occupy. Jericho stood in their way. To cut a long story short, the Israelites won the battle and "destroyed with the sword every living thing" in Jericho.

If this story were just a description of what an army did in a battle that would be one thing, but the problem is that the Bible account claims that those doing the killing were acting for God, that this is what God wanted them to do.

What are we to make of this? Can we call a book that justifies the deliberate killing of men, women and children, a holy book? This is a serious question. What can we say?

Several points can be suggested:

- The fact that we find these accounts problematic shows that we believe that some things ought not to be done. This suggests that we live in a moral universe and this in itself is a sign of the reality of God.

- The God of the Bible is described again and again as a God of love, mercy and justice; a God who is slow to judge and punish. The Israelites did not believe that you could just kill anyone; they worked within a moral framework. The Bible accounts try to give moral reasons for these events. They are seen as carrying out God's judgement against false and harmful religion, against wrongdoing and even child sacrifice. It is said that God had been very patient and had given the people involved a long time to change their ways.

- These events took place a very long time ago and should be judged against the standards of the time rather than by modern standards. For their time, the Israelites were relatively enlightened. Perhaps these military actions were unavoidable at the time. Was this the only way the recently freed slaves could survive in a violent world?

- The Bible is an unfolding and developing story. Earlier views give way to deeper and truer understandings as the Bible progresses. The amazing thing is that the history of the Israelites with its violence and bloodshed eventually gives rise to the one who lifted our sights to a higher vision. In those early days enemies were hated but now we hear Jesus say, "Love your enemies and pray for those who persecute you."

# Forgiveness

Someone has said that 'forgiveness is our deepest need and our highest achievement'. Jesus put forgiveness at the heart of his manifesto when he made it central to the prayer he taught his followers: 'forgive us our sins as we forgive those who sin against us.'

Some of the most impressive acts of human goodwill involve forgiving others who have hurt us or wronged us in some way. This is one reason why Nelson Mandela is so admired. After twenty seven years of imprisonment by a racist regime he was able to put aside hatred and generously forgive.

Forgiveness is liberating. By forgiving we free ourselves from the destructive bitterness that can eat away at us and we also free the person who has done wrong by releasing them from the condemnation we could hold against them.

Central to the Christian message is the claim that we all need God's forgiveness if we are to enter into a friendship with him. This implies that sin alienates us from God and is a problem that each of us needs to face up to.

By 'sin' we might mean particular actions such as lying or stealing or gossiping, or we might mean particular emotions and attitudes like jealousy or selfishness.

Sin could be seen as falling short of what we could be. It might be failing to do something we ought to have done.

The famous story of Adam and Eve illustrates several ideas about the nature of sin. They give in to temptation and they disobey God's command, but at a deeper level the story is talking about trying to replace God by putting yourself at the centre of things. By taking the forbidden fruit, Adam and Eve were saying, 'We're not having God tell us what to do, we are going to do it our way.' Sin in this sense is telling God not to interfere because we are going run our own lives by our own rules, not by his.

Sin is failing to let God be God. It is failing to love God with our whole heart and falling short of the command to love others as we love ourselves. 'I' is at the centre of the word and sin is putting 'I' at the centre of my life.

Perhaps the worst thing you can do to someone is to ignore them or to treat them with indifference. By doing this we tell the other person that they do not matter, that they have no value. God is most hurt, not by particular things that we do, but when we live as if he does not exist.

Some would argue that this is all very well, but sin is only imagined and not real. They would say that our behaviour is not really our responsibility and so sin is not a moral issue. Everything in the universe is caused by something else. Every effect has a cause. My behaviour is not really a matter of choice. Everything I do is caused by my genes, my upbringing and my circumstances. According to this kind of determinism, we have no free-will and, therefore, we cannot be praised or blamed for who we are or what we do. We simply do what our genes, upbringing and circumstances cause us to do.

The Christian faith claims that this is not the whole truth. We are self-conscious and we can stand back from our genes, upbringing and circumstances and make real decisions about what to do and what kind of person we want to be. We all experience this kind of decision making and it is this freedom to choose that makes us able to do the right thing or to fall short.

Some would question the reality of sin because of our evolutionary history. Evolution has given us selfish instincts without which we would not survive. It is this self-centredness that produces competitive, selfish, proud and jealous attitudes and actions.

Again, there is truth in this. We have basic instincts, but again this is not the whole story. We can choose to give way to these instincts or to rise above them. Sin results when we fail to rise above our animal nature in order to live fully human lives.

The Christian faith challenges us not to be naïve and to recognise that sin is a real part of human history and experience. All of us suffer from the sin 'virus' to a greater or lesser degree. We are all born into a human race that has already gone astray in many ways. We all

131

fall short by doing wrong or by neglecting to do the right thing, because of weakness or through our deliberate choices.

We can deceive ourselves into thinking that this is not our problem. A football team can think they are good until they get promoted to the Premier League and then they realize that perhaps they are not as good as they thought they were.

But does it all really matter, is it really that important?

We all confirm in our everyday lives that sin does matter. It matters to us if someone steals our things, it matters to us if someone hurts us by their selfishness, it matters to us if someone lies to us.

Thankfully it matters to God too.

Imagine a God who created the world but then did not care about cheating or lying or killing or racism or selfishness or gossip or greed. If God is good he must care about these things, he must set himself against them. A totally good God cannot say that a little bit of bad does not matter. Imagine a God who said that a little bit of stealing or lying is acceptable. If God is worthy of the name he must set himself against all sin, however big or small.

When it comes to being on good terms with God we therefore face two realities: we all sin and God is against sin.

So, we have a problem. Sin is real and sin is serious.

The surprisingly good news is that God has taken the initiative to resolve the problem. He has taken the sin of the world upon himself in the death of Jesus on the cross.

God can offer us forgiveness because the reality, consequences and penalty of human sin have been carried by Jesus. God has not overlooked human sin, he has treated it with deadly seriousness. And to prove that sin has been defeated Jesus carries our sin to his grave, leaves it there and rises again.

Sin is real, sin is serious and sin is dealt with through the death and resurrection of Jesus.

Forgiveness is our deepest need and God generously meets this need.

Our part is to trust in and to receive his gift.

# Connections

# The Invitation

*Someone was having a huge party and they invited many guests. They sent out the invitations, but to their surprise, those invited all made excuses. The first said, 'I've just bought a house, and I must go and see it. Please excuse me.' Another said, 'I'm buying a new car and I'm on my way to test drive it, so I won't be able to come.' Still another said, 'I'm meeting a girl for the first time, so I won't be able to make it.'*

*The person giving the party was very disappointed, but rather than cancel they decided to go out into the city and invite all of the homeless people instead. Even then there was still room so they went out again and after searching, found more people to come in so that in the end the party was full.*

I wonder why the Bible does not set out a clear set of arguments for the existence of God. You might have thought that you would find a clearly stated, step by step case that establishes that God exists. Yet in all of the Bible's many pages, there is little attempt to prove the point. I wonder why?

Let me suggest that the answer is this: God is not an idea to be debated but rather a person to be known.

Rather than laying out a set of arguments, the Bible records the stories of people who responded to an invitation; the invitation to enter into a friendship with

God. The point is that God is known in the experience of a relationship not as the conclusion to an argument.

There might be people who make lists of arguments 'for' and 'against' entering into friendships, but this is not how relationships normally work.

Relationships involve risk. In friendships we take steps of trust not always knowing how the other person will respond. We involve the other person in our lives, we give time and attention and we talk and so a friendship grows.

The surprising claim of the Christian faith is that the God who made the universe wants a friendship with you and me. He offers us an invitation and awaits our reply.

## The Impossibility of Agnosticism

Being permanently agnostic becomes impossible if faith is seen in terms of a personal invitation.

If someone invites you to an event, or more importantly to be their friend, you might be unsure at first. This is fine as a temporary position, but there will come a time when 'I don't know' in practice means 'No'.

If I remain permanently undecided about a party invitation, I have effectively turned it down.

All of us live as if God is real and important, or as if God is insignificant and irrelevant.

We might want to remain agnostic and say 'I don't know if God is real', but this can only be a temporary position. If this is our long-term response, it ends up being the same as atheism.

# Bowing

*There was once a carpenter who was skilful at making wonderful things with wood. Some people said that there had never been a carpenter like him ever in the whole history of the world. He had a very rare talent, a gift for turning ordinary pieces of wood into beautiful and magical things.*

*Many people loved and admired the Carpenter but strangely some people rejected him, perhaps it was jealousy because people came from miles around to see the things that the Carpenter made.*

*One day the jealous people turned on him and challenged him – 'If you're so clever see what you can make from this.' And they threw at him two ugly and rough pieces of wood nailed together in the shape of a cross. The carpenter lifted the wood onto his shoulders and carried it back to his workshop and everyone waited to see what he would make.*

*The next day the Carpenter came back and said, 'It's finished!' And they said, 'So show us. What have you made?' And the carpenter said, 'You gave me some ugly wood in the shape of a cross and I have worked on that wood and made it into the frame of a door. And if you go through that door you will find yourselves in a joy-filled and wonderful place. If you go through the door that I have made you will enter into Paradise itself.'*

*Some of the people laughed. 'How could a carpenter turn an ugly cross of wood into a door that leads to heaven?' But others were curious and said, 'We'd like to see this door that you say you've made.' And so the Carpenter fetched the door and stood it in front of them.*

*When they saw what he had made they were taken by surprise because the door was very humble and low, so low that you would have to bow down to go through it.*

*And some people said, 'You don't expect us to get on our knees to go through your door do you?' And the Carpenter said, 'You gave me a cross and I have turned it into a door into heaven. You are all invited in!' But some turned their backs and walked away. And the Carpenter saw them turn and go and he looked at the ones who were left and he said, 'Do you want to go too?' And they said, 'Where could we go? Where else would we find a carpenter who can turn a cross into a door that leads to heaven?' So they bent their necks low and passed through the door that the Carpenter had made.*

*Words cannot describe what they found on the other side, but I can tell you this: they had no regrets and they were so glad that they had trusted the Carpenter and bowed down and walked through the door that he had made.*

# Speaking

A friend accepts us, trusts us, cares about us and will be loyal to us. A saying out of Africa says, "Hold on to a true friend with both of your hands." Loneliness is an unhappy place to be; it feels good to have friends.

Abraham lived nearly 4,000 years ago and yet his story is still read, told and pondered by three of the world's religions – Judaism, Islam and Christianity. It is a story about a journey of faith that took him from belief in many gods to a deep trust in one God. A journey from ancient Iraq to the land of Canaan, the part of the world we call Israel. In that story we find Abraham described as God's friend. It is an amazing claim. Could it be true that the God who created the universe wanted to be in that kind of relationship with Abraham; that God wanted to be Abraham's friend?

Abraham's story continued through his descendants and Moses was later to be another key figure. And in the story of Moses we find it again, we are told that God communicated with Moses just like a person speaks with a friend. Abraham and Moses were friends with God. And this turns out to be the theme of the Bible story – the God who made us wants us to know him as a friend. It is a mind-blowing thought – the possibility of an eternal friendship with our Creator.

We all know that if our friendships are to survive and deepen we need to invest time and energy in them and the same is true of a friendship with God. One of the key ways that friendships grow is by communication. We communicate with our friends in all kinds of ways.

So how can we communicate with God?

Praying is talking to God and it builds our friendship with him as well as changing us in the process. Life can be hectic and busy, but if we take some time each day to be still on the inside as well as on the outside, we can get in touch with the fact that we have an inner life (a spirit) as well as a body. This can help us to be a calmer, more together person and at the same time our friendship with God can deepen and grow. We can thank God for the good things of life and we can ask for his forgiveness. We can talk to him about the things that make us angry and the issues that are worrying us. We can speak about people who are facing difficult times and we can ask for help. When we pray, we know that if God is our friend he will listen to our prayers. When we ask for things, he knows much better than we do the best way to answer. A good and wise friend can be trusted but such a friend will not always say 'yes'.

Praying does us good because it stops us getting locked into a frantic life-style in which we forget who we really are. It gives us a chance to re-focus our lives, to be thankful and to be thoughtful. It broadens our minds and our horizons. And by praying we can help other people and engage in the needs of the world by talking with God about them. And if we talk, our friendship with God will grow and, as we pray, we will sense that God is real and not far away.

**Try an experiment:**

Find a quiet place and get comfortable.

Try to be still inside and out.

Trust that God is listening.

Tell him how you are feeling, the positives and the negatives.

Say thank you for the good things in your life.

Think about and name the people you care about.

Say sorry and ask for forgiveness.

Be still, calm and peaceful.

# Listening

If we can communicate with God by praying, how does God communicate with us? A one-way friendship does not get you very far. We need God to speak.

Christians make the exciting claim that God has made himself known in the past and that he continues to communicate with people today.

So how does God speak to us?

He might guide us through the advice of wise people or the promptings of an informed conscience.

He might reveal himself through the beauty of the natural world. Wherever we come across truth, beauty, love and goodness, God is there.

Many people would claim to hear his voice as they meditate on the message of the Bible.

The first half of the Bible (the Old Testament) tells the unfolding story of the Jewish people and their struggle to know and love God. The second half (the New Testament) is about Jesus and his followers and the very early days of the Christian faith.

The Bible is not however just a record of the past. We can experience God speaking to us today as the Bible is explained to us or as we read it and think carefully about it for ourselves.

The Bible is a diverse collection of books, originally written in Hebrew and Greek by several writers over a period of many years. The ideas develop and grow. The insights of later writers expand and sometimes replace those written earlier.

Some of the books are letters written to help people facing particular issues and questions, others are history or prophecy or the lyrics of songs or poems.

To understand the Bible we have to take into account the type of book we are reading and the time, place and culture in which the authors were living.

We can also ask questions about manuscripts, sources and dates. Another interesting area is archaeology. This can help us to examine the historical claims of the Bible.

Sometimes it is not easy to see what the writers are getting at, or to know how to apply what they say to life today. Understanding the Bible requires an effort on our part and we might need help, but the effort will be worth it if we are able to hear God speaking to us as a result.

The best place to start is with the life and teaching of Jesus recorded in the Gospels of the New Testament. Jesus lived two thousand years ago but God still speaks today through the example of his life and the wisdom of his teaching.

If we take the time to reflect on the message of the Bible we can experience God speaking to us. We can discover what God is like, what he thinks of us and what he expects of us.

If we are willing to listen and to think, we will hear God's voice.

**Why take the Bible seriously?**

- It addresses deep questions
  about ourselves,
  God and the world.

- It can give us
  wise advice and guidance
  for life.

- It helps us
  to look critically
  at today's beliefs and attitudes.

- It has great stories
  with heroes and anti-heroes.

- It has inspired
  millions of people.

- It has changed
  the world.

- It has stood
  the test of time.

- It is a best seller.

- It is a collection of books
  through which God speaks.

**Try this experiment:**

Find a Bible and look up 'The Gospel of Luke'.

Expect God to speak to you.
Adopt a humble attitude and open your heart.
Say a prayer asking God to speak through what you are about to read.

Read a short portion.

Think about what you have read and ask what God might be saying to you.

\*

Read a short portion every day.

\*

Once you have read some of Luke's account, choose a particular story and try to imagine yourself as one of the characters. What do you see, hear and feel?

\*

Find a Christian group where the Bible is explained and discussed. Go and listen and join in and see if God speaks to you.

# Receiving

The Christian faith can get stuck in lifeless rules and dead rituals, but it can also be a living, empowering and dynamic force in a person's life.

Jesus said that God will respond like a loving Father, if we come to him like a child and ask him to give us his energy, his Spirit.

This dynamic presence of God's Spirit in our lives can make God real to us. God feels like a close and loving Father rather than a distant idea. God becomes more than a concept to be discussed and debated. He can be known and loved.

The power of God in a person's life can help them to follow Jesus' teaching and makes living as a Christian much more than being 'religious' or merely trying to obey rules and exercising will-power.

As we open ourselves to God we gradually change and become more like the person we want to be. We grow good 'fruit' in our lives. The New Testament says that, 'the fruit of the Spirit is love, joy, peace, patience, kindness, goodness, faithfulness, gentleness and self-control.'

The earliest Christians are said to have experienced the power of God coming upon them. The story is told in terms of purifying fire and a powerful wind: a fire that burns away the things that hold you back and a wind that drives you forward.

It is possible to be filled up with the Spirit of God. This is like filling a car with fuel. You cannot run on an empty tank and you have to fill up often.

Being a Christian is a dynamic and living experience.

Many people have found that when they ask for God's help and make time to open themselves to his Spirit, they experience something new happening in their lives. God starts to be more real to them and they begin to change. They become spiritually alive.

**Try this:**

Find a quiet place where you can relax and know that you will not be disturbed.

Put things right with God. Ask him to forgive you for any wrong things you are aware of. If necessary go and put things right with anyone you have hurt. Tell them you are sorry and ask for their forgiveness.

Be willing to forgive anyone who has hurt you. This might not be easy. Speak to God about what happened and why you feel hurt. Ask God to help you to forgive. Pray for the other person that God will make things good for them.

Relax and take time to be still. Let go of the things that are on your mind.

Tell God that you need his help. Ask God to fill you with his Spirit. Open yourself up to God.

Jesus said, 'Ask and you will receive.' Trust that God has heard your prayer.

Pray to God like this often.

# Belonging

If you have ever watched a coal fire burning you will know that an individual piece of coal soon goes cold if it is left on its own. While it is in the fire it burns brightly, alone it dies away.

The Christian faith is not meant to be lived alone. Faith is kept alive and grows when it is explored within a community of believers. In such a community, a person can hear the Bible discussed and explained and they can find God speaking to them. In such a 'family' it is possible to connect with God in worship, in prayer and by receiving the bread and wine as Jesus' last meal with his friends is re-enacted. Special times of the year like Easter and Christmas also take on a particular significance as the high points of the Christian story are relived together.

In this kind of community, people gain strength by sharing their struggles and using their gifts and resources to help each other.

Being a Christian is not just about individuals believing certain ideas. It means belonging with other people who are learning to know God better. It is about knowing God with friends who also want to grow in love for God and for others.

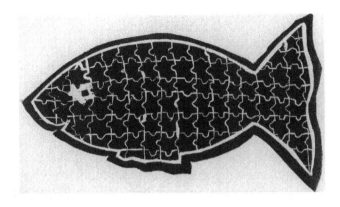

*Adela*

Christian churches are made up of people from all ages and all kinds of backgrounds. It is an amazing thing to be part of a community that might include business people, pensioners, teachers, those with special needs, doctors, students, farmers and factory workers.

This means, though, that the Church is made up of ordinary human beings and so, not surprisingly it has weaknesses and failings. Despite this, many people find that belonging to such a community of faith helps them as they try to learn what it means to love God, to love each other and to reach out with love to other people.

To keep your personal fire of faith burning you need to spend time with others who are burning with the same fire.

Is there a local community that you could join, a church where you could connect with God and with others?

# Doing

Actions speak louder than words.

Jesus said that some people would hear his teaching but fail to put it into practice. They are like someone building a house on a sand dune. The foundation is unstable and the house will not survive the storm. Putting Jesus' teaching into practice, builds your life on a solid foundation. It is about doing, not just knowing; actions not just words.

We come close to God when we get involved in his work in the world.

We see in the story of Moses that God cared about the political and economic oppression of people who had been forced into slavery. Through Moses God liberated them and led them to freedom.

We see Jesus' compassion as he feeds the hungry, heals the sick and brings comfort to the troubled and bereaved.

The main way in which God works in the world today is through people who will play their part in his purposes.

God is looking for those who will care enough to give their time, prayers, money and talents to make a difference.

None of us can change the whole world but we can all change the world for someone.

As we care for those around us and commit ourselves to peace and justice in the wider world we come close to God and we bring God close to others.

Jesus said, *"I was hungry and you gave me something to eat, I was thirsty and you gave me something to drink, I was a stranger and you invited me in, I needed clothes and you clothed me, I was sick and you looked after me. I was in prison and you came to visit me."*

What will you do?

What difference will you make?

# The Stone

*A wise woman who was travelling in the mountains found a very precious stone in a stream.*

*The next day she met another traveller who was hungry, and the woman opened her bag to share her food. The hungry traveller saw the precious stone and asked the woman to give it to him. She did so without hesitation.*

*The traveller left, rejoicing in his good fortune. He knew the stone was worth enough to give him security for a lifetime.*

*But a few days later he came back to return the stone to the wise woman.*

*'I've been thinking,' he said, 'I know how valuable this stone is, but I give it back in the hope that you can give me something even more precious. Give me what you have within you that enabled you to give me the stone.'*

*(Original author unknown)*

# The End

Can you think of any situation in which the practice of unselfish love would not be the right thing to do?

Love is the final reality.

The Christian faith makes the bold claim that beyond the fundamental particles of matter there is a God of love. At the heart of the universe there is a God who cares about us, a personal God who loves us and longs for a response of love from us.

This love became flesh and blood and was made visible for us in the life and death of Jesus. Jesus shows us a strong, determined love; a tough rather than sentimental kind of love.

It is hard to love like that. We need God's help if we are going to live in the selfless kind of way that Jesus lived. With God's power, with the help of the Holy Spirit we can begin to learn to love like that.

And so we can speak of love to the power of three. The Trinity:

- Behind all that we see is a Father God who is love.
- Jesus, the Son of God, shows us what it means to love.
- The Holy Spirit of God can give us the power to love.

Questions or comments?

Get in touch:
friendship.god.faith@gmail.com

Printed in Great Britain
by Amazon